Wolf in Sheep's clothing

I see myself as a person at war, and the battle is against evil, and the weapon I am using to defeat my adversary is the pen. My aim is to dispense, as much as I possibly can, the truth in regard to the nature of my nemesis.

There is an expression which very much describes my present circumstance, and how I am able to do what I do: "Keep your friends close, and your enemies closer". I am quite literally in the trenches, on the battle field, surrounded by my enemy.

Lives are lost every day in the mine field deployed by those who are sick and depraved beyond belief; ask any of those who witness the same as I, and you will, practically without exception, not be told anything about what they have seen and heard, or a claim will be made that they have seen or heard nothing.

The logic behind this behaviour, to make an analogy, is as follows; if I've been involved in the commission of a crime, and live off the proceeds of that crime, why would I say, or do, anything that would have a tendency to incriminate myself; for instance, mentioning any knowledge of a bank heist.

The various criminal acts detailed throughout my writings that take place in Canada, and are perpetrated by Canadians, are done in order to insure they may be able to acquire cash without having to do any actual work.

Canadians, generally speaking, are far too lazy to make the required effort to meaningfully educate themselves; as long as they are able to get whatever they want, whenever they please,

The Trinity Manifesto; Vol. I

I'd like to acknowledge the immeasurable, incalculable, support of an unseen entity guiding me, helping me, and protecting me, as I was putting together this book.

I've been blessed to have experienced over the span of just a few years enough drama, excitement, intrigue, mystery, suspense, tragedy, and despair, to fill a thousand reels of film that would constitute the greatest Hollywood epic ever made.

While in the midst of these affairs, completely out of the blue, the first two lines of a poem would appear in my mind. As soon as possible I would furiously write down the rest.

"Love Is the Nature of Existence", stemmed from the ideas planted in those poems, polemics, and tales; most of which I have left unedited; they remain the same as when they suddenly sprang into my mind. Where they came from, heaven only knows – literally.

Art can be defined as the realization of what is imagined, such being the case, the words contained in this book will awaken the possibility for a new beginning, a rebirth, a chance for a continuation in our collective struggle to survive.

The Holy Spirit never left my side;
in fact, He is here with me,
and always will be.

Love Is the Nature of Existence

Nigel Shindler

The Eternal Journey

This book is dedicated to all those who made history.
Your number was so few, but without each one,
Nothing else would have been possible.
Thanks to God all mighty,
The one who chose
Them all.

ALSO BY
NIGEL SHINDLER Ph.D.

Love Is the Nature of Existence
VOLUME II
Love is The Word and the Time is Now

Love Is the Nature of Existence
VOLUME III
Trinity
The Father, the Son, the Holy Ghost

Love Is the Nature of Existence
VOLUME IV
The Creator

The Boy and the Tower
The
Memoirs of
Nigel Shindler

The Trinity Manifesto; Vol. I

CreateSpace
4900 LaCross Road
North Charleston SC, 29406
Copyright 2000-2013
CreateSpace, a DBA of On-Demand Publishing, LLC
www.createspace.com

ISBN-13: 978-1500236021
ISBN-10: 1500236020

CONTENT

Love Is the Nature of Existence

CONTENTS
Love Is the Nature of Existence
VOLUME I
The Trinity Manifesto

List of Poems

List of Illustrations

The Trinity Manifesto; Vol. I

Now there are times when a whole generation is caught…
between two ages, two modes of life, with the consequence
that it loses all power to understand itself and has no
standards, no security, no simple acquiescence.

Herman Hesse, *Steppenwolf*

…it is silly
To refuse the tasks of time
And, overlooking our lives,
Cry -- "Miserable wicked me,
How interesting I am."
We would rather be ruined than changed,
We would rather die in our deed
Than climb the cross of the moment
And let our illusions die.

W. H. Auden, *The Age of Anxiety*

Foreword

e live in a world of stark contrasts that should give us all cause for concern, and wonder how such things arose.

Some among us are enormously rich, while a great many others live in abject poverty. Those who work the hardest, producing the most, typically earn far less than those who spend an inordinate amount of time consuming products they play no role in producing.

We have an immense array of renewable resources at our disposal, yet we continue to heavily rely on non‑renewable, carbon based substances, such as oil and gas, that have spawned climactic changes on a global scale we should find alarming.

It is easy to determine that if we continue to follow our present course, it is inevitable we will cease to exist as a species; we will also jeopardize the survival of every other species on this planet; an increasing number of which become extinct every year.

"Love Is the Nature of Existence" explains the evolutionary process that has led to the formulation of these events. The truth is being hidden by a lie, and the orchestration of this lie is used as a means to acquire wealth. The level of exertion devoted to the manufacture of this lie, is proportionate to the perceived threat of the truth being exposed.

I am most fortunate to presently reside in Canada, where there is practically no expended effort to camouflage the truth. I'd like to reveal the truth as to how Canada procures its wealth; it doesn't! The government states that its citizens are consumers, and no attempt is made on the part of Canadians to refute this claim.

Canada proclaims to be a country that honours Human Rights, and, therefore, encourages refugees from around the world to immigrate to this country.

The truth is that Canada allows its population to feed on the portion labelled as "marginalized". In order to conceal this savagery, Canada doesn't mow its victims down in front of firing squads, or place them in gas chambers, rather it systematically deprives the marginalized class the basic necessities of life; all the while asserting they are offering assistance to those they intend to place in a grave.

The primary instruments employed to conduct this genocide are those who proclaim to be "oppressed" themselves; women in particular. People have been "trained", I prefer the expression, "programmed", to perform as a collected body to conceal the truth.

Among all the cities I have resided in Canada, Ottawa, I would have to say, extends the least effort to disguise the fact its population consists entirely of consumers.

The business/commercial district of the city is flooded with stores, and shortly after the "work day" has finished, practically all the stores close.

Because the population has little else to do but consume products, any sort of meaningful education is quite redundant; however, an extraordinary percentage of Canada's population acquire some form of post-secondary education; a certificate, diploma, or degree; yet only a minute sector has even a rudimentary grasp of the fundamentals required to speak either English of French proficiently.

Quite a large chunk of Canada's immigrant population makes no attempt to learn either Canada's national languages, or make the slightest exertion to learn how Canada's political/bureaucratic systems operate. Why would they when their sole purpose is to consume products!

For such a horrendous state of affairs to be possible, and on such a massive scale, Canada has resorted to using its population as a shield to block others from discovering the truth. Over time people repeat the lie so often they eventually believe it to be true; which is made all the easier due to the extent of its magnitude.

Due to the truth being so self-evident in Canada, I managed to figure out why our world is in such a terrible state. People have become an amalgamation of ingredients coagulated to form a product designed in accordance with social engineering projects that have been in operation since the Second World War; heavily relying on propaganda campaigns identical to those exercised by the Nazi Regime.

The overall prime directive has been to insure the rich get richer, while exerting themselves less and less; thereby guaranteeing those responsible for implementing this scheme needn't expend any energy whatsoever to secure their wealth.

One shouldn't, therefore, find the video tapes of Rob

Ford, Toronto's Mayor, surprising. He was elected by the people of Toronto, and despite being a, crack smoking, beer swilling, gluttonous, hooligan, who cannot differentiate the artistic merit between a Shakespearian Sonnet and a Marvel comic book, remains the mayor of the city.

"Man is the only creature that consumes without producing.
He does not give milk, he does not lay eggs, he is too weak to pull a plough, he cannot run fast enough to catch rabbits. Yet he is lord of all animals. He sets them to work, he gives back to them the bare minimum that will prevent them from starving, and the rest he keeps for himself."

George Orwell, *"Animal Farm"*

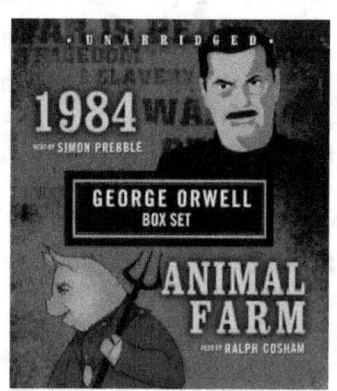

Introduction

he primary role of the Canadian public within the Monolith's scheme is to spend money, as much of it as possible, and within the smallest expanse of time, thereby insuring the orchestrators of the Monolith acquire wealth themselves, and without the slightest expenditure of energy.

Canadians consume, they do not, generally speaking, produce, and the education system insures none, or at least very few, will ever have anything to offer society, especially something that could manufacture a "culture"; enrich the minds of others.

Money is placed in the hands of the Canadian public by using the I.D. of the Marginalized Class to transfer funds. Members of the Marginalized Class are deliberately denied the Right to be independent and self-sufficient as a result; coming off social assistance would mean a loss of revenue for Canada's consumers.

In order to achieve this objective the Canadian people openly perpetrate the most heinous crimes imaginable; much unlike Nazi Germany where a large portion of her population declared after the Second World War they did not know, were not aware, of the atrocities that took place in the Concentration Camps. There is indeed much evidence that Hitler and his henchmen went to great lengths to hide from the general public the mass exterminations that took place in these Camps.

The goal of the Monolith is to make sure money arrives in the hands of those predisposed to use money carelessly, and neglectfully. Those inclined to use money to enrich their minds are the last among the population to be granted any form of wealth.

Canada's lawlessness can been defined as a condition of "hyper-democracy", which also explains how the state of affairs came about. People over the course of several decades, (this is a global phenomenon, Canadians are simply the most extreme form), were granted liberties, and have, in manner of speaking, given into their human nature, (I prefer to think of it as submitting to sin, or taking the bait), and consequently lost the ability to have a conscience; the ability to feel guilt, shame, regret, or remorse, while inflicting unfair, unjust, pain, and suffering, upon others; the result is the bizarre world we live in today; one in which people believe everybody can, and ought to be, equal, (the aim of democracy is the promotion of individuality, every person being given the opportunity to reach his fullest potential, which is the opposite of the tyranny of hyper-democracy).

We should all be allowed equal opportunity, but one would hope that some will excel in their chosen field, and be able to develop something others can value, and appreciate, as exceptional. "Hyper-democracy" discourages such behaviour, the very thing that enables a society to be sustainable, and flourish; this is self-defeatist, and will, ultimately, lead to the obliteration of a civilization.

Canadians make no attempt to hide the fact they believe they have the Right to force individuals to conform to the "norm" – neither rising above the "proper" level, nor allowing them to lag below. People, literally, punish those who are advanced beyond the norm; this is considered proof of an "undemocratic" superiority of actual ability; no individual is deemed to have the Right to achieve a superior level of achievement; in fact, anyone demonstrating the existence of such a capacity is judged to be "antisocial", and should be punished for his "criminally undemocratic" actions.

What one could call, lopsided superiority, can be tolerated to a certain degree; in other words, a person with a high I.Q., may also be afflicted with, for example, Parkinson's disease, and receive a measure of support, (a brilliant cripple); a form of "equalization" is manufactured in the mind, resulting in the person being perceived as average instead of superior; a genius without a physical or mental handicap of some sort is, on the other hand, "unacceptable". To suggest that individuals who are genuinely, innately superior is, in the "hyper-democratic" society, a concept that is intolerable.

Regarding my own circumstance, I have been denied a post-secondary education in Canada, and furthermore, have regularly been denied Public Library privileges, usually by fines being made up.

Love Is the Nature of Existence

When a person goes to a physician, typically, it's because something about their physical well-being isn't to their liking, or something might be wrong; it isn't functioning as it should, or at its optimal level. An appointment is made, and a meeting will take place in an office of some sort.

Wouldn't you consider it strange if a physician took his practice outdoors, and instead of waiting for people to approach him, he informs those who pass by that they require his assistance.

There is little doubt in my mind that the vast majority of people would consider such a physician to be a "crack pot", and in need of medical assistance himself. If anybody needed to reassure himself that what he was being told wasn't true, he could just glance around at his fellow man to notice that there was little to differentiate him from others; but therein resides the problem, and the issue at hand.

To make an analogy; if I were to greet someone, and say, "Your boots need cleaning; they're covered with dirt"; the person might then turn to the one beside him, and take note that the colour of their boots is the same, and happens to know they both bought their footwear at the same store; and, therefore, might feel entitled to ask; "What on God's green earth are you talking about?"

I could then respond by saying; "If you wipe your boots with a cloth, you'll notice they're the colour green, not brown; you've continually been stepping in filth."

Such is the state of our world today; pretty much everybody is walking around in a haze; perceiving neither themselves nor their surroundings lucidly; thus, having little appreciation of how one affects the other.

In order to make such a person aware of his circumstance I have to lessen the fog, which means I have to affect the faculty generating the fog, which is the mind of a person that is actually unable to recognize a fog even exists. I have to, therefore, somehow heighten the mental acuity of the person who isn't thinking lucidly.

One method I can use to achieve this objective is to be frank, open, direct, and to the point; instead of skirting the issue, which was actually the tactic used to confuse in the first place; the objective being, to provide just one example, to acquire information without the person being aware of how or why this is being done.

For example; a man has lost his watch, and wants to know the time, but without others becoming aware he no longer has a time piece. He might greet someone and say, "I didn't expect to bump into you here; I thought you had a meeting." The other person answers; "The meeting finished a couple of hours ago." He then knows the time is approximately three, because the meeting was supposed to be finished at one: But what would be the point of continually manipulating a person in such a manner?

It could be considered fruitful for someone wanting to know the time, without having to invest money in purchasing a watch. The best scenario for a person who refuses to not invest any time, money, or effort, in keeping track of the time of day, is to sit in a chair, do whatever he pleases, and whenever he becomes curious about the time, all he has to do is snap his fingers to insure someone approaches and provides the information he desires.

How could such a scenario possibly appear normal to someone with a time piece, and cognizant that his sole purpose in life is to provide the time to someone without a watch of their own? What an empty and senseless way to live one's life!

A day consists of 24 hours, and if one uses time wisely a lot can be accomplished. For instance; many believe in order to master any discipline, the guitar, for example, 10,000 hours is required, regardless of the extent of one's "natural talent".

A most common scenario these days is as follows; someone might claim to have mastered the classical guitar because he believes he's as talented as, "Joe Blow from Kokomo", who happens to be nowhere near as accomplished as Christopher Parkening, whom he's never actually heard, due to never having had the time; or so he believes.

The haze is created by people, literally and figuratively, running around in circles, while engaged in the most mindless, senseless, endeavours one could possibly imagine, and, consequently, depriving themselves of the opportunity to become aware of how damaging, and self-defeating, such behavioural patterns are.

"Love Is the Nature of Existence", is the cloth that can wipe away the dirt that has accumulated on ones' boots, so that one can become aware of the magnificent footwear one's been wearing all along!!

The Trinity Manifesto

If one were to consider, "Love Is the Nature of Existence", a symphony, it consists of four movements, and the overture happens to be Volume 1, "The Trinity Manifesto". The whole is encapsulated in answering the question; what is the nature of the being Man has become?

Most describe Man in accordance with his outward features, but if one were to measure his value by observing his patterns of behaviour, he can no longer be seen as a creature having dominion over all others, but rather a cretin that has sunk so low he now, figuratively speaking, resides in a cave; a sub-terrain abode devoid of life, and any resource that can furnish his mind; but he isn't cognizant of this because there isn't an opening for light to enter, and therefore no contrast exists to reveal how deep the darkness is that surrounds him; he doesn't even foresee his surroundings as being dark because there's no light to expose this fact.

Despite the immense amount of knowledge that has been granted mankind throughout the eons, predictions have persistently been made by those possessing the finest minds that collectively our nature will inevitably plummet. Why is it their visions of the future have consistently been so incredible accurate? Considering the plethora of resources available to enrich ourselves, how it is people continually manage to lead themselves astray? So often people seem far more inclined to pursue self-destructive pursuits, rather than follow a path that will enhance a skill, and fulfill their potential.

If one were tumbling down a hill, heading for certain doom; why wouldn't such a person latch onto an outstretched hand offering help?

The key to answering this question is recognizing the possibility that the person who's life is in jeopardy is unaware of such being the case; thus, the hand granting assistance isn't perceived as a "way out", but rather an obstacle hindering one's passage; up is now down; down is up; right is left; left is right; backward is forward; forward is now backward.

A person can only have the opportunity to recognize that his mode of living is the reverse of what it should be if something ministers as a contrast to expose this being the case.

One way of keeping those who constitute the masses ignorant is by eliminating the existence of anything that counters a position commonly believed to be true. For example; cheese will be foreseen not to have holes; if no one is given the opportunity to proclaim there is such a thing as "Swiss" cheese.

Why would someone be stifled from stating the truth? One reason could be that one wishes others to fill in the holes they've been told don't even exist, which would insure the cheese is not shared among those placed in such a position; they are not interfering with the consumption of a product.

If one's objective is to accumulate wealth, a common method is to train people not to disrupt the currents followed by capital; they can, in fact, be used as a devise to enhance the flow of funds; which happens to explain how and why Man has become the lowest life form.

If a person were to become aware of the tragic nature of his condition, he might feel compelled to alter his state of affairs. The easiest way to avoid such a circumstance is to annihilate the opportunity for an acknowledgment to develop.

Contrary to the manner people tend to perceive themselves, none have been manipulated against their will, but have voluntarily followed a course resulting in them being trapped in a cave.

One would think it would be rather difficult to persuade a person to reside in a place that is cold, dark, and damp, as opposed to a warm, and sunny, Mediterranean beach, (the world today in contrast to the Garden of Eden) - actually, it's not that difficult at all. Picture a person crawling along a tunnel hoping to reach a treasure chest believed to have been abandoned centuries ago. The allure is an object that doesn't exist; the attraction is the suggestion inspiring the person to believe the treasure can be discovered by searching for a light flickering off the surface of shiny gold coins, in a place where light has no chance to even reach; in other words, their actions are conducted in accordance with their delusional beliefs.

The aim of, "The Trinity Manifesto", is to remove the patches covering people eyes, so they are able to realize they are not planted in a cave, but, rather, what lies before them is the vision of a field of golden grain stretching as far as the eye can see.

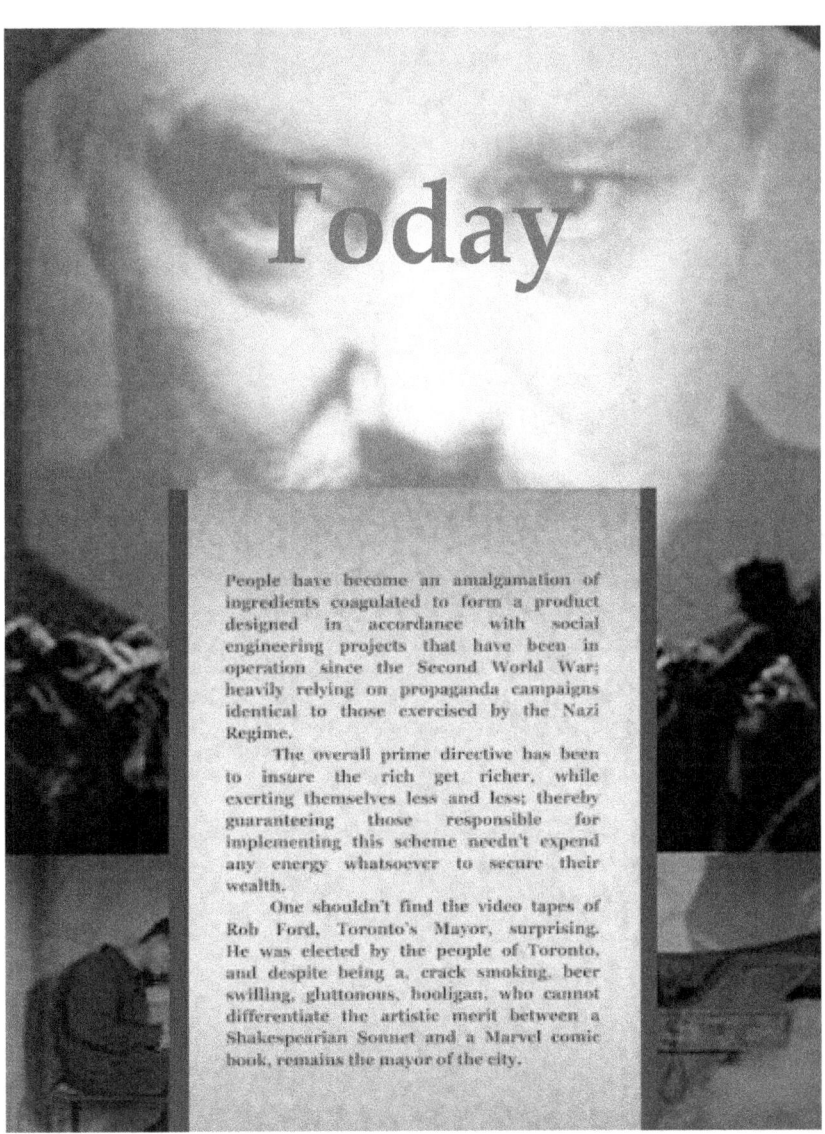

Today

People have become an amalgamation of ingredients coagulated to form a product designed in accordance with social engineering projects that have been in operation since the Second World War; heavily relying on propaganda campaigns identical to those exercised by the Nazi Regime.

The overall prime directive has been to insure the rich get richer, while exerting themselves less and less; thereby guaranteeing those responsible for implementing this scheme needn't expend any energy whatsoever to secure their wealth.

One shouldn't find the video tapes of Rob Ford, Toronto's Mayor, surprising. He was elected by the people of Toronto, and despite being a, crack smoking, beer swilling, gluttonous, hooligan, who cannot differentiate the artistic merit between a Shakespearian Sonnet and a Marvel comic book, remains the mayor of the city.

Karl Marx

Every self-alienation of man from himself and nature appears in the relationship in which he places himself and nature to other men distinct from himself. Therefore religious self-alienation necessarily appears in the relationship of layman to priest, or, because here we are dealing with a spiritual world, to a mediator, etc. In the practical, real world, the self-alienation can only appear through the practical, real relationship to other men.

Thomas Jefferson

Shake off all the fears of servile prejudices, under which weak minds are servilely couched. Fix reason firmly in her seat, and call on her tribunal for every fact, every opinion. Question with boldness even the existence of God; because, if there be one, he must more approve of the homage of reason than that of blindfolded fear.

George Orwell, "1984"

"For, after all, how do we know two and two make four? Or that the force of gravity works? Or that the past is unchangeable? If both the past and the external world exist only in the mind, and if the mind itself is controllable – what then?"

"Power is not a means; it is an end. One does not establish a dictatorship in order to safeguard a revolution in order to establish a dictatorship. The object of persecution is persecution. The object of torture is torture. The object of power is power."

The Trinity Manifesto; Vol. I

was it a novel, a year?
Or a time
to face the truth?
Man had chosen the wrong path;
the end was now near.

Ever since man has been corrupted;
this has been the case with each passing year.
The evident consequence is an increase in fear.

The horrors that fill the world are so many,
but few are mentioned;
why bother when you have a comfortable pension?

Computers have brought this destruction.
Patience has been lost.
Man acts through illogical compulsion.
The focus to do what is "good" has been diminished.
My God! It's over; we're all finished!

What more is there to say?
A dear price it is we now pay.
Increasingly we lose the potential to feel gay.

So few are aware of how total is our nightmare.
Those that do, number so few; they are extremely rare;
        the cost has been due to being totally unfair.

PBS NEWSHOUR; WHAT DO YOU THINK IS MORE IMPORTANT FOR KIDS; HARD WORK, IMAGINATION, OR FAITH?

THE WORDS FAITH, HARD WORK, AND IMAGINATION, I'M SURE, HAVE A PERSONAL MEANING FOR EVERYONE, WHICH CAN ALSO CHANGE OVER TIME; THEREFORE, I CANNOT ANSWER THE QUESTION BECAUSE I HAVE NO FRAME OF REFERENCE.

I DO FIND IT CONCERNING, HOWEVER, THAT PEOPLE ARE INCLINED TO MAKE PRESUMPTIONS ON SUCH MATTERS, WHICH CAN ONLY LEAD TO MISUNDERSTANDINGS, MISCOMMUNICATION, AND, THUS, HAMPER ONE'S EFFORTS TO ACCOMPLISH AS MUCH AS POSSIBLE DURING THE DAY, (WHICH CAN BE EXPRESSED AS "HARD WORK"; WHICH CAN ALSO BE EXPERIENCED, OR PERCEIVED, AS ENJOYABLE DUE TO HAVING A SENSE OF WORTH AND MEANING).

I IMAGINE, (THE WORD IS A CONSTRUCT MANUFACTURED BY MY MIND, BRAIN, SPIRIT, ENTITY, BEING, MAYBE ALL, AT OTHER TIMES POSSIBLY NOT), THE TERM "FAITH", FOR MOST, IS ASSOCIATED WITH THEIR RELIGIOUS, IDEOLOGICAL, AND CULTURAL, BACKGROUND, THEREFORE, UNLESS I AM PROVIDED INFORMATION ON SUCH MATTERS, I COULDN'T POSSIBLY FORMULATE AN OPINION; I CAN, HOWEVER, SPOUT OUT A PREJUDICIAL REMARK, WHICH IS A COMMON FORM OF BEHAVIOUR AMONG THOSE INCLINED TO BOOST ABOUT HOW MUCH THEY KNOW.

A COMMON PROBLEM IN OUR WORLD TODAY IS THAT MOST BELIEVE THEY ARE SAYING SOMETHING, WHEN, IN FACT, THEY ARE SAYING NOTHING AT ALL, ("DOUBLESPEAK", "NEWSPEAK").

Day 1

W e, in society today, take it for granted that we are members of the species Homo-sapiens, within which there are five primary classes, or classifications; they are not, contrary to popular belief, separate Races. The word "Race" can most simply be defined as a group of persons having a common ancestry. No matter the class a person is stated belonging to, the ancestry is common among all, and this is most evident within our genetic makeup.

The classes have arisen due to the outward appearance which distinguishes one from the other, and has developed as an adaptive mechanism to environmental conditions. To make a comparison, I may be the owner of an expensive watch that I like to have on my person as I go about my daily affairs. In order to protect it, and insure it remains in good working order, I can take various measures to achieve this objective. I could have it encased in something that I unfold when I want to view the time, I could make sure its tucked under my sleeve as much as possible, so as to protect it from the elements, I could have it attached to a chain, for example, and the watch is kept in my pocket, and I simply tuck on the chain when I wish to extract it. No matter the means used to extract the watch, or where the watch is kept on my body, the manner in which the watch functions, and the components that make up the watch, remains the same.

Until a few decades ago, all watches were mechanical in structure, and there would be a knob, to give just one example, a person would turn in order to keep the parts moving, so the hands on the face of the watch could tell us the time. Once, so called, electrical watches, came along, a battery of some sort, would commonly be placed inside, and this in turn would generate activity within the watch, which makes the hands on the face move around a central pivotal point, or it might have a display of numbers that change at a constant rate, serving the same purpose.

If I may make an analogy of Man being much like a watch, we each must learn about the mechanisms that enable it to operate, so as to sustain our existence. We may, for example, learn by imitative and repetitive behaviour how to turn the knob ourselves, or place a battery inside. If we lack the manual dexterity for a time to do these tasks ourselves, someone might do this for us, and later, when the time is right, when sufficient physical skills, and mental aptitudes, have been assembled, we can independently preserve our existence.

The watch (Man) is not unlike any other species on this planet; it not only wishes, and is driven, to sustain its own existence, but that of all watches as well, therefore, it must procreate in order to achieve this objective; and there is a similarly constructed watch that enables this to transpire. The completion of this task is achieved once a watch is capable of sustaining its own existence; being independent, and self-sufficient, in other words.

The question remains; when can a watch no longer considered a watch? The answer lies at the conclusion of the last paragraph; such being the case, do we see evidence of this in Man's behaviour; which is, no doubt, a product of the society in which he is situated? My answer, most definitely, is YES?

Our genetic ancestry is, indisputably, connected to the Ape family; there is very little that differentiates us from gorillas, orangutans, and baboons, for example. The brain appears larger than others included in the Ape family, in proportion to the size of the body, which, in my opinion, helps to explain the creation, and use, of various tools over the Ages that has helped sustain Man's existence. We have a cerebral cortex that appears slightly more developed than Apes.

For countless thousands of years, Man existed primarily as a wanderer, having little contact with members of his own kind; if groups did develop, their number might be counted on the fingers of both hands.

Eventually, Man discovered "agriculture", which managed to provide a more secure source of nourishment to maintain the operation of each "watch". This led to people collecting and forming groups in order to cultivate wider stretches of land, which managed to increase the amount of time one could devote to scholarly pursuits; at the same time, due to the change in the milieu Man inhabited, measures had to be undertaken to protect him from the others who comprise society - namely, other watches.

In order for him to be able to go about his affairs, and not have to be continually vigilant of the other watches, laws were established, and each watch was required to comprehend the nature of these laws; not just to sustain his existence, but to have the opportunity to make it a nourishing, rewarding, experience.

Man is a creature, after all, that acquires a sense of security, and comfort, by learning to control, and utilize, something outside of himself; what better tool does Man possess than his mind, (this is what differentiates Man from other members of the Ape family), to fulfill this task.

Societies are not, and have never been, entities that exist in complete isolation; for example, agricultural civilization is commonly thought to have begun in Mesopotamia, but had to fight off incursions made by barbarians from the east; Mongoloids. The Mesopotamians, due to available "recreational" time, and accessible resources, began to develop what we refer to as "culture".

I use this word in a Germanic sense, rather than the various descriptions that are typically attached to the concept today; it is not simply table etiquette, social etiquette, the manner in which food is prepared, rather the nutrients that enable the watch to work more proficiently, or possibly acquire a capacity previously unknown, or undeveloped – say the aptitude to predict the next lunar eclipse; mere procreation does not enable such proficiencies. Culture, to me, means; a repository of human knowledge, artistic brilliance, and the search for human perfection · these are the ideals, and the properties that provide the potential for it to be manufactured.

For a man to become cultivated, (some prefer the expression, civilized), what components are necessary for this undertaking? In order to answer this question I will again compare Man to a watch.

The watch is placed in an ecological system that it must navigate appropriately in order to survive. It must learn the laws that govern the society it operates within, and the society protects itself from elements that can compromise its capacity to survive; intruders, (barbarians), for example, and make efforts to insure the proper use of elements within nature so as to make sure they are a reliable, sustainable, source of nutrition; if water is diverted to nourish a field, for example, another man's land must not be compromised by a lack of available water, and so on and so forth. Man, thus, must learn to be moral; he must take care of himself, whilst not compromising the welfare of another, (do unto others, as you would have them do unto you).

The best way a man can assure he doesn't harm himself is by not harming anyone else. One very effective way of teaching this is that when it does occur, (an infraction of the law), the individual is extracted from the society so no further damage can occur, and hopefully, by being deprived of things he once had, and the pleasure derived from them, he will not repeat the same conduct again. It is, therefore, essential that each person within society have the tools available to achieve this objective; is there evidence of this being the case in the world today? Civilizations have developed throughout the world since the time of Mesopotamia; surely we should have learned the essential lessons by now.

The simplest way of answering this question is by analyzing the stages of development, viewing it as a linked chain, much as one attached to a watch one keeps in a pocket; if any link is weak, this would compromise the integrity of the entire chain, and the purpose it is meant to serve; for door number 2 to be opened, one must first pass through door number 1, to arrive at step number 2, first one must place a foot on the lower step, alternatively entitled, step number 1.

For the continuing existence of all watches to be feasible, the male watch mates with a female, and the new watch must attain the skills required to sustain his existence, which entails the development of an understanding of his general makeup, thereby ripening an awareness of the resources available within himself that can be utilized. For such to be possible, the new watch, whether male or female, must learn to get along with his mother and father, in other words, cultivate morals that he/she will later adhere to within the wider scheme of society, (honour thy mother and father, is one of the ten Commandments). This is where we notice the manner in which Man differs from what we commonly consider our closest ancestor, the Apes.

Mammals and animals, have what can be called "instincts", they assure its capacity to survive, which includes morals; other species as well appear to keep checks on their behaviour so as to insure their survival; they eat when they are hungry, drink when they are thirsty, etc., etc.; in other words, there is a balance in their overall behaviour, they live within their means, and do not overindulge. These faculties appear to apply to all mammals and animals. They also over time learn more and more about the environment in which they are situated, in order to acquire the nutrients essential for their survival; this faculty could be called their "ego".

Man appears to be lacking in such natural restraints, therefore, the mother and father must teach such things, until, hopefully, they indeed become a part of his/her makeup. The new watch wishes to sustain its own existence, and must develop the capacity to acquire the abilities I have mentioned; how does such occur?

First, the new male must not harm the source it requires to learn essential skills; and obviously, the parent male/female must learn about the nature of the new watch, so as not to harm it. Fortunately, included within the male is the capacity to develop moral behaviour, Sigmund Freud called this the "Oedipus Complex". He, the new male watch, is naturally drawn, attracted, to, simply put, the first object from which he acquires the nutrients that help sustain his existence - the mother. Due to a lack of learned moderation, he wants, desires, the mother all to himself, and, therefore, perceives the father as his rival. He must, to insure his survival, learn to overcome this disquieting state of affairs in his mind. The role is also to assure his most vulnerable body part is not placed in jeopardy, from which he also has the capacity to derive much sensory pleasure; thus, a fear develops that his father might severe his penis, testicles, or both, as a form of punishment. When a resolution is ascertained, moral behaviour will be the evident result.

The new female watch develops in a divergent manner; her attraction is to her own mother; where is her vulnerable body part? Who is her rival? Unlike the male of the genus Homo species, she is dependent on the environment to instruct her as to what is correct, proper, just, and fair. A greater challenge is placed on the parents to instill moral behaviour in the female because she is unable to develop such capacities alone.

The learning process is longer, and slower, as a result, and is acquired principally by having an example to imitate and emulate; which, quite obviously, is her mother. It is due to these factors that the male is, thus, innately superior to the female, and this is why The Bible instructs the "male" to dominate the "woman", (eastern mystics, customarily, describe man as being the highest form of evolution). Sigmund Freud stated that men create history, and history reveals this statement to be true; the Jews, God's Chosen People, are not merely primarily males, but are, without exception, men.

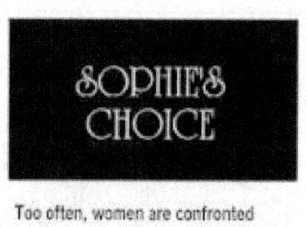

Too often, women are confronted

The challenges we face in life are the very things that make us better; which would explain how some tend to view difficulties not as unwarranted, unjust, obstacles, but blessings; in regard, to women, one can confidently state that they, as a class, have not been given proper consideration, and that's putting it mildly, and society, human civilization, as a whole, has paid a very dear price as a result.

Once either the male or female acquire the ability to maintain checks on their behaviour, a "superego", has been manufactured, and then, he/she can be considered belonging to the genus Homo.

Man's instincts can be called the "id", the manner he incorporates himself in any ecological system is due to his "ego", the "superego" keeps the "id" in check, so as to keep him safe, thereby better insuring survival; denoting, not harming himself; signifying, understanding his own nature, not harming another, and generally keeping moderation in all affairs.

Animals and mammals, appear to not require the growth of a "superego" beyond conception, therefore, I should capitalize their "Id" in order to differentiate it from Man's basic instincts. One way of understanding this better is by picturing a train running along tracks, at a certain point along those tracks they become slippery, and its brakes are far less effective. To protect the train, and not compromise the safety of the passengers, a contraction is implanted to force the train to slow down; obviously, if the train is travelling at a rate of speed that is too high around a turning, it could topple over, potentially having catastrophic consequences.

Animals have the necessary brake mechanism already implanted; the male/female watch must manufacture it in order to survive. It can, thus, be concluded that for a society to function, be self-sustaining, and eventually acquire the capacity to develop culture, a "superego" must be incorporated in the new watches, both male and female.

In my opinion, I have just addressed the root cause of all the problems we are facing in society today. It has been constructed to hinder, in every way possible, the capacity for a person to become human. There are many that now claim our education –system has a dehumanizing effect. I think the terminology used is incorrect; by not developing a "superego", we, as a species, become "savage primates" – we continually harm ourselves, and one another, some to such an extent they are entirely unaware of this, and if they are, they do not care, which means they are not immoral, but amoral; they do not question if something is right, wrong, good, bad, or take a moment to consider the possible consequences, and repercussions, of their actions, in the near, or distant, future.

Thank you, say the corporations, we got exactly what we wanted; while the earth crumbles and disintegrates all around us.

Seven Deadly Sins

Wealth without work
Pleasure without conscience
Science without humanity
Knowledge without character
Politics without principle
Commerce without morality
Worship without sacrifice

"When I despair, I remember that all through history the way of truth and love have always won. There have been tyrants and murderers, and for a time, they can seem invincible, but in the end, they always fall. Think of it -- always."

"Live as if you were to die tomorrow. Learn as if you were to live forever."

"Happiness is when what you think, what you say, and what you do are in harmony."

"A man who was completely innocent, offered himself as a sacrifice for the good of others, including his enemies, and became the ransom of the world. It was a perfect act."

"Mahatma Gandhi"

Gandhi

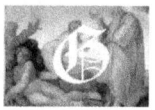 *andhi had such lofty ideals;*
they soared to such heights,
few of us, with all due
respect, could possibly achieve.

Bent and weak, he could often be;
walking with a cane
he could often be seen;
despite all this
he was a man Leaders would flock to see.

Independence for India he desired.
He and that land, we realize now, were as
        one.
He fought till the right
to chart its' own course had been won.
Many seekers had the same desire,
but few like Gandhi
were prepared to burn on a pyre.

Self-sacrifice for Mohandas was a gift;
to offer oneself for a cause you sought to
        lift.
You have thus not been taken away,
but added to a pursuit to make others
        sway.

For all these things, he did so earnestly
        pray.

Man

 hat makes a man?
Many things of a kind we
do not understand.

Days pass,
  we are awake,
and when we close our eyes, we sleep.

Through it all we have a journey we must
    follow.
The answer to it all, we always hope, will
    happen in the morrow.

We search, we follow, until we can
find shores of solid ground we can call our
    own.
Some call this our final resting place;
others consider it home.

No matter how far, or how fast, we travel,
no time has passed.
We will always end up where we are now.
The beginning is the end.

The question many ask is; how?
Trying to understand all this
can sometimes send us around the bend,
but still we pursue the quest to
    understand;
though, from one day to the next,
we appear no closer to the truth,

The Trinity Manifesto; Vol. I

to the Promised Land.
Could it be we need a helping hand?

The search without will make us weary.
Finally, we search within.
We develop a new theory.

The ultimate is obtainable;
true knowledge of everything that has
  been,
and everything we could possibly see.

The complexity of ourselves,
is daunting to comprehend.
Layers, stages, rungs, stepping stones;
the essence of our being goes deep into our
  bones.

There, we can say,
everything outside is a reflection of what
  we have within.
What is it we avoid most?
Is it fear?
It inhabits unknown territories guarded by
  a shadowy host.

We fear ourselves;
the truth that lies within.
We should ask ourselves;
can we stand the truth, or will we fall,
  and never rise again?

Oh, the pain!
Existence is merely a game.

The Trinity Manifesto; Vol. I

Let's end it,
and free ourselves from all suffering,
for all time.

The Buddha said it all.
Many Giants there have been,
but he stands among them all as the most
    tall.

CAGE OF FREEDOM
Jon Anderson

Cage of freedom
That's our prison
Where the jailer and the captive combine
Cage of freedom
Cast in power
All the trappings of our own design
Blind ambition
Steals our reason
We're soon behind those invisible bars
On the inside
Looking outside
To make it safer we double the guard
Cage of freedom
There's no escaping
We fabricated a world of our own…

Cage of freedom, growing smaller
'Till every wall now touches the skin
Cage of freedom, filled with treason
Changing sides as the loses begin
Our suspicion tries escaping
But they set up the security
There's no exit – there's no entrance
Remember how we swallowed the key?
Cage of freedom, that's our prison
We fabricated this world of our own…

Big brother
Is there a bigger one watching you
Or is there one smaller
Who I should be watching too
Infinite circles of
Snakes eating their own tails
For everyone chasing
Another is on their trail

Is that a friend
Can you tell, is he on your side?
'Cause I spy with my little eye
Yet another spy....

IS MORE IMPORTANT FOR KIDS; HARD WORK, IMAGINATION, OR FAITH?

PBS NEWSHOUR
 WHAT DO YOU THINK IS MORE IMPORTANT FOR KIDS; HARD WORK,
IMAGINATION, OR FAITH?

PUTTING ASIDE THE FACT THAT EACH OF THE WORDS, FAITH, HARD WORK,
AND IMAGINATION, HAVE VARIOUS DEFINITIONS, AND MEAN SOMETHING
PARTICULAR TO EACH INDIVIDUAL DUE TO THEIR OWN IDIOSYNCRATIC
CULTURAL BACKGROUND; WHAT DOES THE WORD "KIDS" MEAN? FOR
EXAMPLE, WHAT AGE GROUP IS BEING REFERRED TO? FURTHERMORE, WHY
IS IT AN "ADULT", IF THAT IS WHOM THIS QUESTION IS MEANT FOR, THAT
IS UNABLE TO ASK THESE SIMPLE, FUNDAMENTAL, QUESTIONS,
DETERMINING FOR ANOTHER HUMAN BEING WHAT IS MORE IMPORTANT?
 SUCH MINDLESS PREOCCUPATIONS FILL UP A LOT OF PEOPLE'S TIME, AND
THEY ACTUALLY THINK THEY ARE ENGAGING IN SOMETHING IMPORTANT;
THIS IS MORE OR LESS WHAT IS HAPPENING IN OUR SCHOOLS TODAY, AND
"ADULTS" ARE SETTING A VERY POOR EXAMPLE FOR THEIR CHILDREN.

 ALICE IN WONDERLAND
 IS ALICE LIVING IN WONDERLAND, IMAGINING WONDERLAND, OR IS
WONDERLAND ACTUALLY HERSELF; A PROJECTION CREATED BY HER MIND?

**❝ If I had a
world of my
own, everything
would be nonsense.
Nothing would be what
it is, because everything
would be what it isn't. And
contrary wise, what is, it wouldn't be. And
what it wouldn't be, it would. You see?**
Alice in Wonderland

Day 2

n Day 1 I raised the question; is Man a member of the genus Homo? My conclusion was that by observing the manner in which he behaves, it is possible to discover whether the mammal, commonly referred to as "human", is a civilized being; denoting, having acquired a "superego"; or, on the other hand, is a "savage primate", otherwise called a "brute", due to an inability to restrain his "basic urges", (also labelled "instincts").

I also stipulated that we are unlike all other mammals, who appear to have an inborn, inbred, conscience, or "superego"; meaning, the ability to curtail modalities of behaviour within certain parameters, which acts to help sustain their existence.

I concluded that the "system" presently in place is constructed to insure that the capacity to develop a "superego" is severely compromised, if not entirely eliminated. The question I will tackle in Day 2 is why this is the case? Day 3 will deal with the question of how it came about.

The "system" today is most commonly labelled "Globalization". The word, "system", according to "The Little Oxford Dictionary of Current English", compiled by George Ostler, (third edition, 1941), is defined as follows: n, complex whole; set of connecting things or parts; organization; method; (principle of) classification. What is essential, in reference to Globalization, is that everything is integrated to serve a particular purpose.

My claim in "Love Is the Nature of Existence" is that the entire operation of this system is for the benefit of a minute portion of the world's population; they are responsible for its design, implementation, and are the primary beneficiaries.

Rome wasn't built in a day, and neither was the global economy we have now. The title I apply as a means to describe the people at the top of the totem pole, so to speak, that garner the greatest proceeds from this system, is the word, "Monolith". This word according to the above mentioned dictionary means, n. single block of stone or pillar. They, however many they might be, are solely responsible for sustaining the system; although, peculiarly enough, nobody, as far as I am aware, knows who these people are that collaborated to build, maintain, and reap whatever benefits there might be from planting this structure in our world.

The consequence of such being the case is that people, generally speaking, believe they are in control of their destiny. To make a comparison, as a means to explain how such a mentality develops; a man can only operate if he is given the proper time to rest in order to, in a sense, recharge his batteries. He believes this will occur while he is, to provide one example, asleep, unconscious. What he is unaware of, however, is that there is a little man that hides under his pillow, and turns a dial a certain number of times, in a counter-clockwise direction, that is responsible for the man becoming re-energized; therefore, it is not a state of unconsciousness that enables the man's internal mechanisms to obtain nourishment, rather the sleep state enables the body to remain in a motionless position that better enables the "dial man" to accomplish this task.

In other words, people believe they are running their own show, because they cannot detect any evidence that there is a director running the production; which reminds me of the movie, "The Wizard of Oz", where the Wizard manages to hide behind a curtain until Dorothy pulls it aside unveiling the identity of the conductor.

The world today is, as pretty much anybody will tell you, run by money. A person obtains money, then spends money in order to acquire objects that he believes will enrich his life, and enables him to lead the lifestyle of his choice. "Money talks", is a commonly used expression today, and most are inclined to believe that the greater amount you have, the more gratifying, and rewarding, your life will be; "everyday can be a good day", (whatever that happens to mean).

It is very easy then to see the world as a business; producing and selling particular products. People are needed to make products, other people transfer these items, (whom I call collectively, "salespersons"), into the hands of those whose primary purpose in life is to consume goods. There are, thus, essentially two different types of people in the world; 1) Producers, and; 2) Consumers, (those responsible for transferring the saleable items do not in any way play a role in the production of the goods they handle, and therefore, I include them in the category of Consumers).

Our globe is covered with patches of land designated as countries; the Producers primarily reside in those labelled as the Third World, while the Consumers, for the most part, reside in the nations labelled as the First World.

There is no longer a Second World, for all intents and purposes, which contained the Communist World, and that has enabled, in a manner of speaking, the oil that lubricates the parts that make up the system to flow more readily.

Due to the labour required to manufacture goods, one might believe it is logical to assume the population with the most money would reside in the Third World; after all, shouldn't everything be earned, and receive fair compensation – surely, this is the very essence of what justice means. This is not, however, the case; the wealthiest (Consumers) tend to reside in the First World; which does make sense when you consider that in order for them to do their "Job" money is required, and the more money you have, and time available to utilize the products bought, greater is ones' success in behaving as a Consumer.

One could picture this scenario as follows; twenty people spend a third of a day preparing a sumptuous meal for a party of four. The diners have little else to do with their time, so they are in no hurry to finish their meal. Once they get through their final course, they notice, (to give an example), lunch time has arrived, and they begin eating their next meal, which the group of twenty people in the kitchen have been labouring to prepare while the people seated at the table have been eating their meal. Occasionally, the people that work in the kitchen might have the opportunity to quietly sneak beneath the table, and find a few crumbs to contain their hunger; if one is lucky, he might catch a bone thrown aside that still has a sliver of meat attached, and a bit of gristle; this is a heavenly sight in comparison to the collection of crumbs he can gather between two fingers.

Quite a contradiction isn't it! Those who do the most labour, receive the least amount, monetarily; those deserving of the most gratitude and appreciation, are the ones that go about mostly unnoticed; on the other hand, those who offer the least, are the ones actually receiving the most. One can assuredly conclude that within this scenario everything is operating in the opposite manner one would expect, and common sense tells us it should.

This would indeed be the case if ones primary concern was the betterment and wellbeing of all concerned. Those that run the "Shop", however, are in no way included in the operation I have just described. They are somewhere outside of the business where the exchange of goods and services is transpiring.

It is fair to conclude that those who constitute what I call the Monolith, are driven in the same manner practically everybody else is; actually, this is the furthest thing from the truth. Money is required to buy objects, that is a given, and, without a shadow of a doubt, one requires money to make more of it. Even if you are one who spends practically the entire day standing in a field picking coffee beans, one requires money to buy the food needed to perform labour. How does the Monolith acquire money despite being neither a Consumer nor Producer?

The answer is simple to explain; picture the following; a man enters a restaurant after a long day at the office to enjoy his dinner. While he is still considering what he should select from the menu, a gentleman approaches, and in a soft, but pleading, voice, asks if he might be able to spare a bit of change so he can buy a little food to help fill his stomach that has been empty all day. Due to finding it rather difficult to ignore his plea for assistance, and wanting to enjoy his meal in peace, and also have a sense he is a good person, who helps the needy whenever presented the opportunity, he reaches into his pocket and extracts a couple of bills, and hands them over – all the while overwhelmed by the extent of his generosity. The beggar in return expresses his gratitude and leaves.

All is now well, because he can once again return to his menu and make a selection without any more distractions; however, he's much hungrier than he was before, and he believes this is due to his meal being postponed; in actual fact, it is far more due to the sight of the ravenous man begging for help in acquiring a meal of his own.

The Monolith owns and operates the restaurant, but does not have to be present in order to acquire the means to live the lifestyle of their choosing; the primary method used to accomplish this task is as follows, and, I believe, encapsulates the nature of all the techniques currently in practice used to attain funds.

A patron, the same man mentioned previously, opens a menu while seated at a restaurant, and discovers there is only one selection available, and it's a succulent duck roast, (at least according to the ad), smothered in a sauce consisting of four words, and more syllables than he dare attempt to count, and sounds, as a consequence, absolutely delicious; and also quite exotic, so he can brag to his friends later about his extraordinarily unique meal; but wait! There is a problem. The duck is $15, and he only has $10. He could have his meal somewhere else, but how could he ever forgive himself if he allowed this opportunity to have so delectable a dish pass him by.

Fortunately, a remedy is found, when he notices a sign attached to one of the pillars that make up the decor of the restaurant's interior – a loan is available, with interest.

"Bulls eye! Jackpot! My lucky day", thinks the patron. He calls over the waiter, and asks for further details about the loan. He agrees to the terms and conditions, and signs on the dotted line without blinking an eye. It seems like a sweet deal, and he's already salivating in expectation of the duck roast that will soon be on a plate at the table he's seated.

The interest goes into the pockets of the Monolith, and they didn't need a cent to acquire this money. All they required was the man to decide to live beyond his means; all the while believing his actions are reasonable, justifiable, and also considering himself blessed to be presented the opportunity to make the deal.

Believe it or not, it doesn't require much effort to set up the scenario I've just described. If the proper ingredients, in the right quantities, are mixed together, it will repeatedly secure the same reward.

The question remains; is there one ingredient that is absolutely essential, and can be considered of greater importance than all others, and makes everything else, in a sense, run smoothly?

My conclusion is YES, there is, and it is making sure people become brutes, savage primates, and haven't, as the expression goes, any "self-restraint".

People who continually toil, doing repetitive, monotonous, backbreaking, labour, become brutes, due to the continual strain they must endure, and the lack of balance, (variety), in their lives; they are hindered from remaining, or developing into, human beings. Those who continually live beyond their means, (gluttons), acquire the same traits. Narcissism develops, until a point arrives when the person appears to himself to live in his own universe, where every want, need, and desire, should be satiated immediately; an, "I'm alright Jake. Looking out for # 1", mentality becomes evident; but can such a business, consisting of Producers and Consumers, be sustainable? The answer, indubitably, is NO!!

If something is meant to last, it must, in a sense, be self-generating; both the Producers and Consumers within the picture I've illustrated, are living unbalanced, excessive, gluttonous, lives; both, however, believe it is for their betterment. In the case of the Producers it is a means to survive, whereas for Consumers, it means, or so they believe, getting the most out of life.

The truth is the exact opposite in both cases. The "Earth Shop", sometime very soon, will have to close for business, for the simple reason that excess can only eventually lead to disintegration; in much the same fashion that if you play with a toy longer, or more intensively, than you are supposed to, due to either negligence, ignorance, or both, for example, at some point the toy is going to break.

A man is only human when he is humane. Any life that isn't, to use a blanket expression, "balanced", will reveal signs of this in his behaviour. Having stated the previous, what I believe is a commonly accepted fact is that in Third World Countries (TWCs), wherever they might be upon the globe, great injustices are transpiring, and on a scale that is hard to fathom due to the magnitude, and are also quite impossible to ignore.

Most currently have the impression that inhumane acts are greater in these countries than others due to the publicity garnered from the reports of these terrible, despicable, acts of bloodshed. Truth be told, however, and this has always been the case in human history, the worst crimes, the most atrocious, heinous, deeds, are kept secret. People remain silent so as to hide the nature of the act. Once again, reality is in fact the opposite of how the common man typically perceives things.

There is a reason why such a state of affairs has arisen, and it is due to the time the business began to be put together, and the ingredients used to formulate this operation.

I think it is safe to say the world experienced a new beginning following the end of the Second World War, and people had the opportunity to open their stores again for business, and dust off their welcome mats – the time for firing pistols, and throwing hand grenades, was over. The world should have been very cautious in noting that more than a few of the doctors, scientists, and others considered among Nazi Germany's intellectual elite, were allowed to flee, escape trial for their crimes, and instead started their lives anew, and for the most part, in FWCs. The bell over the door that rings once you open it should have sounded like a siren going off in people's heads.

Since the 1950's, more and more people have been moving from one region of the globe to another in search of economic prosperity, or enhanced security, (refugees, asylum seekers, for example), or both; particularly since the mid-1980s when, by coincidence, or design, the first personal computers came on the market.

"Love Is the Nature of Existence", details how it has been the primary instrument used to serve the same purpose as the notice attached to the pillar in the restaurant I described previously. It allows one access to the means to fulfill their every desire; whether it is a duck roast, a new car, a house, even a horse you can keep in the barn you have on your country estate.

As I've already noted, the excesses occurring in the Third World are quite clear to see. The mentalities responsible for such "imbalances" are transplanted to the new homes of the immigrants in the First World.

It is important in order for businesses to run well, (meaning an increase in the amount of money, and merchandize, exchanging hands), that anything that can impede such a flow be eradicated, after all, excess can only lead to more excess; what you want, need, and desire, will be accelerated as well – until eventually what is acquired is an "Instant Gratification Complex".

When one looks at the history of North America, for example, it can be easily noted that the first obstruction presenting itself was the Aboriginal Peoples, and the means used to eliminate this barrier is well documented.

Since the Second World War, the same patterns of behaviour have existed, and the tactics used to accomplish similar objectives, are identical to those practiced in Germany, Continental Europe as a whole, by the Nazi Party; the Nazis did take what they deemed were necessary measures, however, to keep their worst crimes a secret, due to knowing they would cause "distaste" among Germans, even those who openly committed atrocities. The country I'll provide as an example to illustrate this point is the one in which I currently reside, Canada.

Canada is the most consumerist country on the face of this Earth, in my opinion. It has, proportionately, a large immigrant population, (making a comparison with other FWCs); they consist of the very rich and others one could consider deprived – both are unbalanced to an enormously unhealthy extent; and this is the only important ingredient that need be noted.

Due to Canada being a land full of Consumers, the populace is expected, (in order to keep the Monolith happy), to dine, (a colloquial expression for "consume"), as often as possible, and for this to happen, there shouldn't be an inclination to spend countless hours in a laboratory attempting to invent a better light bulb. Endeavours of this nature can only slow down the transfer of money.

Where does a country full of Consumers acquire the cash to buy all the meals it consumes? As one might expect, the TWCs in which Human Rights violations are openly committed.

The intention, and purpose, is very similar to how the Monolith operates; for example, a person opens a "Sweat Shop", but pays the workers sub-subsistence wages, which can only result in a higher profit margin; the proceeds of crime are then transferred to a "central location". Canada consists of 10 provinces, and three territories, and the stolen goods must somehow be transferred to each of these regions; how does it do this in order to reach Consumers?

The answer is simple; in the same manner so called Cowboys dealt with the Indians out West when they were trying to reach gold, and build settlements for themselves; for example, Mr. Wigwam lives in the province of Newfoundland goes "missing", using any one of the tactics utilized by the Outlaws in the Wild West. Canada makes no attempt to hide the fact it does this.

It is interesting to note that Canada not long ago placed a serial killer on trial in the province of British Columbia, and is reported, and proudly claims, to have killed 49 people, (his target number was 50). Most, practically all, his victims were people considered of a marginalized status, (mostly Aboriginal prostitutes).

He left a great deal of evidence over the course of more than a few years that he was slaughtering people, on his pig farm of all places, but the local detachment of the R.C.M.P. failed to detect a whiff of this trail.

The admitted serial killer, Robert Pickton, was eventually convicted on 6 of the cases. A formal "inquiry" was conducted by the R.C.M.P. following his trial, and concluded the following; had they been able to tackle the case all over again, they would not have done anything differently – hindsight of course being 20/20.

Canada enjoys creating the illusion that such atrocities are a "holdover" from an unsavoury portion of its history that it is still struggling to overcome. The truth is far more heinous, deplorable, and atrocious, than most could even possibly fathom. More and more, at an ever increasing rate, Canada is becoming a society seeping with Consumers; thus, more victims are needed to transfer funds in order to provide pay cheques to the least educated, (lacking "proper schooling"), most unskilled – by the way, Canada has developed a reputation of having a legion of taxi drivers that are engineers, doctors, and others with doctorates, due to being unable to find supplementary means to acquire an income.

Secretaries, desk clerks, others with long, fancy, but essentially meaningless, titles, are provided enormous sums of money to do the most menial of chores; but this does make complete sense, because the objective is that they buy, and consume, as much as possible – not spend hours in a library perusing fine literature. Contrary, therefore, to popular belief, once again; the least deserving, least qualified, most inept, acquire the largest cars, live in the most enormous houses, and possibly have more than just a couple of vacations each year in a far of exotic resort.

Those with the least to offer are provided the most to spend. This makes complete sense when you consider that more cash will then be transferred into the palms of those who form the Monolith.

A "good consumer", to use a metaphor, is inclined to spend a considerable amount of time eating breakfast; fortunately, if you should take longer than expected, no one minds you coming in late for work, or someone of like mind will cover for you; lunch time, can be an hour longer than you are normally granted · who's to notice; snack breaks occur whenever you please; and what's wrong with leaving work early because you want to prepare a nice, hearty, meal for your family; and, hey, it's nice to idle away a few hours in the evening at a cafe, restaurant, or bar, "chilling" with friends over fries, nachos, and maybe a few beers. Everybody works very hard, so who doesn't want to take a break from such a busy, hectic, lifestyle.

How does Canada feed such a consumerist way of living? – answer; create a greater number of people who fit the label of marginalized; but, people definitely wish to perceive themselves as good – which means you can't go around herding people together, then using a firing squad to kill them all. This would certainly discourage refugees from coming to Canada in order to flee persecution, and it certainly wouldn't be good for any business owner to be connected to the slaughter of people; so what can be done?

The most effective way in such a circumstance of killing a person is to deprive them the basic necessities; the requirements essential to sustain life. People obtain jobs in order to acquire money to fulfill, at the very minimum, their basic necessities. If one is excluded from such undertakings, it is the opposite of social inclusion; it is "social exclusion". Aboriginal people, for example, are kept on "Reservations" in Canada, and have little access to proper education. They are deliberately excluded from being able to obtain a vast array of jobs. Many, if not most, Reservations lack clean drinking water, adequate housing, leading eventually to one inevitable result – they don't interfere with the flow of money that enables the Monolith to get what it wants!!

If you are not aboriginal, but are considered of marginalized status, the same tactics are used to make sure the cash directed toward the Monolith continues. Your I.D. is used to signify you have a home, and although you don't actually live there, social assistance is sent to this address, which eventually lands in the hands of the local government office, and they create jobs, so money ends up in the pockets of the Consumers.

The person that is deprived of a home, will also be deprived of proper food, clean water, sufficient clothing, medical and dental services, and if he cannot manage to find anything other than a shelter as a residence - if housing isn't acquired, for example, by the acquisition of private funds, churches donations, etc. - the person will inevitably die; of course, not by natural causes. If he breaks the law, and winds up in jail, then there is no hint of a possibility he can interfere with the flow of cash I mentioned before. If he should wind up in a mental institution, the result is the same.

Every tactic used by the Nazis to make people ill, and weak, is used in Canada; tainted food, noxious gases, toxic water, and so on and so forth. I have personally experienced everything declared above, and I have thoroughly explored the nature of such endeavours on a global, and also historical, scale in "Love Is the Nature of Existence".

What I have discovered is that people are easily capable of all I have detailed above, and in the blink of an eye, because they are "Savage Primates". They do not have the brake pads to slow down their own train as it goes around a sharp corner at a high rate of speed. In another manner of speaking, and to be direct and to the point, they have no will power of their own.

Picture what I have said in the following manner; the energy in your body can be viewed as water that is funneled upward from a well, and then travels through the gullies, (water channels), present in society. If a "superego" is present, water can be diverted when the person chooses; the greater the strength of the will, more water can be controlled, and re-directed. Someone without a conscience has no say, (reminds me of the saying, "money talks"), in the direction, or the amount, of water that flows at any given time, and this is why the ducts, gullies, ravines, etc., (colloquial terms for "behavioural conditioning"), through which water is channeled in society are designed in the manner they are. That is why people are not capable of the shame, guilt, remorse, or regret, that should be associated with the activities I have specified; hence, there is no need for reflection, or introspection, and it is quite evident that people are making no effort to control their behaviour, and that is why they see nothing wrong with anything they do, (in fact, they couldn't change any facet of their behaviour even if they wanted).

Day 3 will explore the methods, and devices, used by the Monolith since the 1950's to create the "Earth Shop" we have today.

Karl Marx

"On James Mill", Early Texts, p 192

Credit is the economic judgement on the morality of a man. In credit, man himself, instead of metal or paper, has become the mediator of exchange but not as man, but as the existence of capital and interest. Human individuality, human morality, has itself become both an article of commerce and the form in which money exists. Instead of money, paper is my own personal being, my flesh and blood, my social value and status, the material body of the spirit of money.

Aldous Huxley

"The Doors of Perception"/ Heaven and Hell

To be enlightened is to be aware, always, of total reality in its immanent otherness — to be aware of it yet remain in a condition to survive as an animal. Our goal is to discover that we have always been where we ought to be. Unhappily we make the task exceedingly difficult for ourselves."

Most lead lives that are at worst so painful, at best so monotonous, poor and limited that the urge to escape, the longing to transcend themselves if only for a few moments, is and has always been one of the principle appetites of the soul.

Each person is at this moment capable of remembering all that has ever happened to him and of perceiving everything that is happening everywhere in the universe.

Ray Bradbury, Fahrenheit 451

"Why is it", he said, one time, at the subway entrance, "I feel I've known you so many years?"

"Because I like you," she said, "and I don't want anything from you."

"Stuff your eyes with wonder," he said, "live as if you'd drop dead in ten seconds. See the world. It's more fantastic than any dream made or paid for in factories."

 *was a man
who worked hard;
often till dawn,
eating nothing but
potatoes and lard.
He knew the
answer could only lie in his grasp,
by studying knowledge
that had been acquired in the past.
When all was added up, the
answer was clear,
the sum total of it all was to reduce fear.*

*Man had been kept too busy.
The opportunity to reflect had been denied.
The solution from him, thus, did hide.*

*Excess is a waste; this is something man
has to face.
Living within one's means, allows all
others to do the same,*

The Trinity Manifesto; Vol. I

then no one need feel shame, or go insane
from living on things such as beans,
that makes your stomach feel an ache, and
   much pain.

Man connects more with his fellow man
when they feel they are much the same;
believe me, this refers also to dames.
With the similarities made clear,
the differences become near, and dear.

Revolution

1917

Lenin and Trotsky,
made a change that year.
They looked to Russia,
and decided the Revolution should occur
    here.
Crush the Monarchy,
then the people would be set free.
Following the teachings of Marx and
    Engels was the key.

They'd tried once before,
but due to the times not being right,
there weren't enough who were able to
    fight;
and the outcome wasn't what they did
    like.

But the second time around,
hearts filled with discontent did abound,
      and things were able
        to be successfully turned around.

PBS NEWSHOUR: WHAT DO YOU THINK IS MORE IMPORTANT FOR KIDS; HARD WORK, IMAGINATION, OR FAITH?

ABOVE IS A SERIES OF WORDS THAT GIVES THE IMPRESSION SOMETHING IS BEING SAID; THAT A QUESTION IS BEING ASKED; THE TRUTH OF THE MATTER IS THAT THIS VERY IMPRESSIVE SOUNDING, AND "WEIGHTY", COLLECTION OF WORDS ACTUALLY ISN'T SAYING ANYTHING AT ALL; NO QUESTION IS BEING ASKED?

FOR KIDS...

...FOR KIDS TO DO WELL IN SCHOOL? DOES THIS MEAN ACHIEVE HIGH GRADES?

...FOR KIDS TO DEVELOP SOCIALIZATION SKILL? SOCIALIZE WITH WHOM, WHERE, IN WHAT CAPACITY, AND ABOUT WHAT?

...FOR KIDS TO FIND LIFE A FULFILLING EXPERIENCE? WHO CAN MAKE SUCH A DETERMINATION?

I BELIEVE I HAVE MADE MY POINT QUITE CLEAR, BUT THE SAD TRUTH OF THE MATTER IS THAT THE MESSAGE I'VE CONVEYED WILL MOST LIKELY, IN MORE CASES THAN NOT, MISS THE MARK; MEANING, GO OVER PEOPLE'S HEADS.

THE TERM "NEWSPEAK", MEANS MUCH THE SAME THING. THE NEWSPAPERS OF TODAY APPEAR TO BE TELLING US SOMETHING, WHEN, IN FACT, NOTHING CONCRETE IS BEING CONVEYED AT ALL.

IT'S O.K. TO RUMINATE OF MEANINGLESS, INCONSEQUENTIAL, PROPOSITIONS; BUT WHEN PRACTICALITIES ARE INVOLVED, THAT CAN LEAD TO A NEGATIVE CONSEQUENCE SUFFERED BY OTHERS, WE HAVE A REAL PROBLEM, AND HARDLY A FANTASY MADE UP IN AN IMAGINARY, NONSENSICAL, BUT DELIGHTFUL, LAND.

Day 3

Countdown to Zero

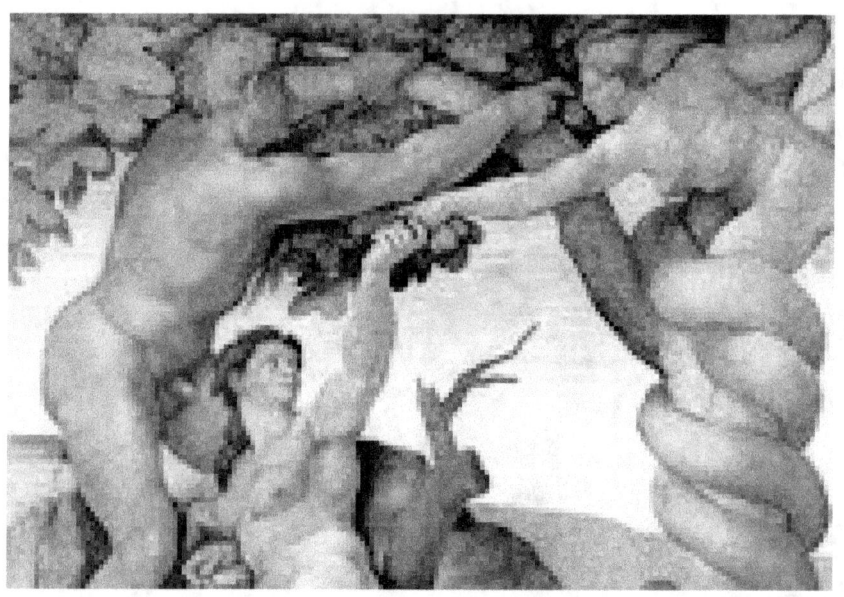

Day 3 answers the question; how did Man cease to be human?

Before I detail how Man became a brute, I would like to describe the extent to which man practices brutality. I will use the population of Canada as my prime example, and this is simply due to being most familiar with the manner in which the economy of this country operates.

I would like to remind my audience that Canada has obtained a reputation of being a just, fair, and tolerant, society – nothing, however, could be further from the truth; but such self-serving mythology enables it to acquire the people it seeks, in order to have them behave in the fashion the Monolith desires.

One should take note that Canada's provincial laws are, essentially, as I would call them, "quasi-criminal". They are constructed to be of benefit to the overall economy, not protect victims of crime, but rather enable crimes to proliferate.

Picture the following as a means to better comprehend my point; a man wishes to obtain cash without having to exert himself, and also manage to spend such cash in a manner that accomplishes in making him appear to be a law abiding citizen.

Man (A) orders Man (B) to shoot Man (C), and once he is dead, extract the money from his pockets, and leave the loot at a location where he will later pick it up. When Man (A) retrieves the money, he hands it over to a local police station; due to the large amount, someone, inevitably, one would think, should inquire as to its whereabouts.

The police congratulate Man (A) for being a good person, due to fulfilling his civic duty, and inform him that if no one claims the money in thirty days, he will be the rightful owner. Dead men don't walk, or talk, so thirty days later Man (A) becomes a very wealthy man, and apparently due to doing the right thing; delivering proof that honesty does pay after all.

The Monolith, actually, acquires its wealth in a similar manner; they have others do their dirty work, and they get all the proceeds from the crime. No investment of time, money, or effort, is required – it's just a matter of time when they receive it.

The Monolith acquires its' wealth due to people buying products they can't afford, don't need, and are actually detrimental to their health and well-being.

Canada uses the I.D. of people to transfer funds so people can get exorbitant wages, while hardly doing any work; their job, essentially, is to buy products, and use them as much as possible; therefore, Canada, certainly couldn't be a country that has a lot to offer others, and if one were to examine the world economy, and how Canada is positioned within, it would become most evident that more, generally speaking, flows in than seeps out.

The people that are excluded from playing a role in society, are eliminated by the use of various methods, and they are, I'm afraid to say, identical to those used by the Nazi Party – they had such success using them while pursuing the creation of a superior race, why not use the same tactics to make a superior economy; a system in which the wealthy elite are not required to work? What could be more ridiculous than squandering something as resourceful as knowledge!

I'd like to present some details and statistics in order to compare Canada to the Nazi regime – all the while cognizant that Canada's objective is not racial purity, but economic prosperity for the members of the Monolith.

In 1933, a steady expulsion of Jews began from the German economy, and their isolation from German society. In April of that year, Germany enacted the, so called, "Aryan Clause" which lead to the dismissal of Jewish civil servants, academics, and teachers. The propaganda used stated that Jews lacked German patriotism – this lie managed to swamp the truth.

Canada does much the same in regards to the people that have been designated as marginalized, which is a clear violation of the Constitution and the Canadian Charter of Human Rights and Liberties; remarkably, those who perpetuate such acts succeed in looking down, if not despising, those they persecute.

When the Nazis came to power 100,000 businesses were owned by Jews, by 1935 this number had dropped by 25%, by mid-1938, the number was approximately 30,000, or a 70% decrease, by the end of 1938, no businesses were owned by Jews.

In April of 1933, a Law was created to deal with "overcrowding" in German schools. The fixed rate was 1.5% of a school's population could consist of Jews; they were repeatedly subjected to bullying by teachers and students.

Canada simply makes up fines, or charges for non-existent items, so the financially strapped marginalized person won't be able to afford an education. If they choose to contest the made up debt, they will be barred by Security from entering the office that deals with such matters, and might also be threatened with a charge of trespassing.

In 1935 the "Law for the protection of German Blood and German Honour" banned marriages, and extra-marital intercourse, between Jews and Germans; due to most marriages in Canada being determined by economics, a person of marginalized status is considered a "poor catch"; compiled with slanderous remarks, and libelous reports, their chances of finding a partner are made even slimmer – this, obviously, contradicts Canada's laws, but such matters are rarely, if ever, enforced.

The "Reich Citizenship Law" stripped those no longer considered to be truly German of their citizenship; there were two categories; 1) Reich citizens, (Aryans with full

Rights), and; 2) nationals, (who were subject to the racial discrimination of the Nazi Party).

Within Canada, Aboriginal people are not considered Canadians, but rather members of "First Nations". Marginalized People, (MP), are treated as objects, not persons entitled to Rights such as life, liberty, property, the Right to pursue justice, never mind, the Right to pursue happiness - a clear violation of Canadian laws in every regard.

Hitler justified the Laws stipulated above by making the bizarre assertion that they were prompted by the provocative behaviour of Jews, and it was necessary to stop outraged German citizens from taking the law into their own hands. He was "containing a problem".

There were essentially 3 steps Hitler took in his quest to create a purer Germen race;

1) Fictional outrage.
2) Defend German people.
3) Destructive threats against the objects of fictional accusations.

The example I provided of the fake debt being used to exclude the MP from obtaining an education is a most common practice throughout all regions of Canada.

The German state seized the property of Jews, and 1 billion Reichmarks were leveled against Jewish communities; therefore, Jews remained on the edge of society, and survived on funds supplied by Jewish Community Organizations or support from individuals.

What has become a common occurrence in Canada is that a MP might obtain, by some means, an abode, and he is then evicted – no justification is required, or evidence is fabricated to achieve this objective, and whatever he is unable to take with him at the time he is evicted is stolen, or conveniently goes "missing" – no investigation will be conducted in order to retrieve this property.

During the reign of the Nazi Party Germans paid for the transportation of Jews by stripping the last assets from their remaining funds. In contrast, quite often in Canada, the MP will use what little resources he has to defend his Rights against fake, and quite often, the most ridiculous, and absurd, claims.

Presently within Canada the mindset of its population is the same as was once exhibited among Germans in Nazi Germany. I'll use the reported perception of a young girl in Nazi Germany as a means to illustrate how the propaganda campaign led people to perceive, and treat others; "...it lead her to feel that she had to cut off ties with Jewish friends, or be a National Socialist." The historian Ian Kershaw wrote the following; "The road to Auschwitz was built on hate, but paved with indifference."

Canadians have a well-known record of being complacent and apathetic, accepting what they are told without question, and turning a blind eye to any sight that causes displeasure. Personally, I don't believe a person can be neutral; if one doesn't do what is necessary to halt injustice, he is complicit, and equally responsible for the act. The person is actually declaring that it is O.K.

Nazis experimented with lethal injections, and gases, on persons labelled as expendable. This was a part of a selective breeding program to improve the human species. During the Nazi reign 400,000 were sterilized against their will, in their quest to create a superior human race.

In Canada there are locations allocated for psychiatric evaluations for those with pending court cases, where they are exposed to toxic gases in order to make them ill, so as to insure they deserve the title of "certified"; injections are also used to tranquilize patients without reasonable cause. They are also deprived of proper rest by doors being slammed throughout the night. Drugs are prescribed to insure criminal acts continue to be perpetrated, (which is the opposite of the claimed intent), due to the sickness induced by the drugs - they actually exacerbate the very symptoms they claim to alleviate. All these measures are used to insure a person is unable to integrate into society – economics, once again, being the driving force.

None of what I have mentioned is, quite obviously, legal. The drugs prescribed cause serious medical ailments, but the propaganda campaign of "bioethics" makes those who administer these potentially lethal drugs actually believe they are for the patients' betterment. Canada's justice system makes it near impossible to win a medical malpractice suit, no matter the amount of evidence compiled. In November of the year 1933, the "Law against dangerous habitual Criminals" was enacted in Germany, and gave police the power to arrest so called a-socials; gypsies, prostitutes, beggars, chronic alcoholics, and homeless vagrants; they would be held in Concentration Camps.

The people in Nazi Germany's mental asylums were labelled as "useless mouths". They would often have food rations cut, and were frequently killed by a combination of starvation and sedatives; most of the doctors engaged in these undertakings volunteered - once again the goal was racial purity.

Canada makes no apologies in any regard about doing similar things; the abuse in Mental Institutions, never mind homes for seniors, is well documented. A simple easy way of killing an Aboriginal is to wait till he's drunk and then administer a tranquilizer; this will sufficiently suppress the cardiovascular system so as to cause death – the driving force again being economics; a steady flow of cash that eventually arrives in the hands of those who can find nothing better to do with their time than purchase products. Buy, buy, buy, buy, and buy; anything that takes your fancy at any particular time.

Between, 1939-1941, over 70,000 psychiatric patients were killed in 6 secret locations by doctors, nurses, and SS men drawn from Concentration Camps. Canada has openly acknowledged it has a problem with stigmatism; the word, "stigma", in reference to people diagnosed with a psychiatric illness, means "exploitation and degradation".

What does it take to induce such forms of psychopathology? How could such a disease of mind spread to such a horrendous extent? The reason is simple to explain; because it is of financial benefit to the Monolith. Quite often the "subjects", a far more appropriate word than "people", (those who perpetrate these crimes), do not have a conscience, and the acts are driven purely on the basis of pleasing oneself, while having no thought in regard to the well-being of those who suffer due to these criminal acts; in other words, they are disconnected, and de-sensitized; sociopaths.

It is, however, quite conceivable to create a stage on which a person can deprive himself of his own conscience, and a person can also be denied the opportunity of developing a conscience. The manner in which this arises is fully explained in Day 1; the young child's ability to relate in a healthy manner to his/her parents is of paramount importance.

Since the Second World War more and more women have ceased to be "homemakers", and instead occupy positions in the "work force". At first women sought jobs as a means to occupy time, which was due to so many convenience products being placed on the market. Presently, the problem has grown to such an extent, that children are neglected and abandoned in enormous numbers, (both are forms of abuse), while both parents are at "work". A great many parents actually believe that such things as "Baby Einstein" are good for their child, without, however, doing any research to discover if the marketer's claims are correct – ignorance is the root cause of such forms of behaviour. Spanking, as ridiculous as it sounds, is now, for the most part, in most instances, considered abuse; even raising your voice can cause enormous mental turbulence, (or so the "experts" say); a wag of the finger is viewed as a threat to a person's integrity, (according to recent "studies" anyway).

Psychiatry first came about in the 1950's, and today is a thriving, lucrative, business. Practically everybody these days is deserving of a label, (according to the latest

Diagnostic Statistical Manual), and no matter the ailment a person has been inflicted with, there is a tablet specially designed to ease their woes; although any neuro-biologist, neuro-anatomist, worth a grain of salt, would tell you the present understanding of the brain is so miniscule, so minute, as to be practically non-existent – the greater the amount discovered, is followed by the recognition of the increase in what is unknown – yet people believe in such things as a "chemical imbalance", and two neurotransmitters being the cause for practically all "psychiatric disorders".

Have I gone MAD? I'm afraid so.
You're entirely Bonkers.
But I'll tell you a SECRET,
ALL THE BEST PEOPLE ARE.
— ALICE IN WONDERLAND

A weakened mind is more liable to be open to suggestion, thus, the proliferation of drugs throughout society, both legal, and illegal, (marijuana, in particular); which includes, soda pop, "fast foods", beer, cigarettes, excessive caffeine consumption, "energy" drinks, processed foods, and so on and so forth. People persistently watch the same shows on T.V. night after night; view the same movies again and again at their local cinema; listen repetitively to the same sort of music; their appearance is very similar from one day to the next, (this is particularly the case among women);

and an enormous amount of time is spent obsessing over "sports"; for instance, golf, bowling, curling, badminton, hockey, soccer, cycling, etc. - everybody wants to be a "Star" these days! The common objective is to make sure people waste energy, and keep themselves involved in mindless activities that weaken the mind, thus making sure suggestions will be more readily received, and there will be a lack of initiative to question information provided.

The whole process took a few decades, and the result is that practically everybody now has been conditioned to respond to stimuli in the same manner a pigeon is trained to perform certain tasks in order to acquire a pellet of food. The patterns of behavioural modification are not complex. The methods used are a combination of classical and operant conditioning.

> Eve took the bite out of the apple; Adam failed to question
> where it came from.

This evolution has gone on so long, people have lost the faculties of free choice/free will, and the ability to introspect to such a degree they are unaware this has even happened.

Thoughts are due to "pseudo-thinking"; they appear to be their own, but the patterns have been incorporated due to the stimuli they are exposed to; which explains why the speech patterns of people are so alike.

There is a cost that must be paid for living in the manner I have described, which has been entirely due to the Monolith, and has eradicated any hope that the problem can be resolved, (rather it needs to be eliminated); we are, after all, reliant on the Earth, and her resources to survive, but due to the "system" that was planted, there was never any hope that the use of fossil fuels could be replaced with something else, (something sustainable, that would have less of an impact on the environment). More and more pollutants have been contaminating the Earth's biosphere at an alarming rate; alternatives have been disregarded, and what Man, as a species, appears to have entirely forgotten is that we are not just a part of the Earth's biosphere, but we also serve a role in the "Divine Order". It is not, therefore, the Monolith that is pulling the strings of the puppets people have made of themselves, but The Lord who is actually the ruler of the Show. He had a purpose when He created it, which is good! The paradox that now exists in the world I have specified enables The Lord to more clearly conceptualize His own nature, which was the sole objective from the beginning.

We ignored His Laws, commandments, instructions, guidance, cautions, and warnings, and, thus, only mankind can be blamed for all the anguish that exists in the world. The Lord created the story, therefore, He knew the end right from the start; therefore, where is it we can go now?

Everything radiates energy, which over time can have an effect on matter far out in space. The Sun is a mere 8 light minutes away from the Earth; due to the fragile condition of the Earth, and the minimal extent Man has made provisions for a disaster, whether it be a flood, tsunami, or a volcanic eruption, we have, indeed, left ourselves in a very vulnerable position. It is not a matter of "if" a global disaster will occur, but "when". Few will see it coming, though, because there might be a new episode of the Simpsons on T.V. which they've seen at least a dozen times before.

In conclusion, I should unveil the identity of those who constitute the Monolith. It is not the Devil, Freemasons, unseen ghouls, or those who take part in "Black Masses"; you'll find them on Wall Street, and their offices are at the very top of office towers. None of them have brilliant minds, or were granted extraordinary gifts at birth; none are all that well educated beyond their field of specialty. They merely had the ability to do what they did, and decided to initiate the process – the rest of mankind is responsible for all the destruction, despair, suffering, and deaths, which have taken place.

When you look in the mirror, and happen to notice a blemish, label it with the word "stigma". Christ did come to save us from our sins by taking them away; but we all have to pay our dues in life, and through his suffering, which we are responsible for, we were supposed to become aware of our mistakes and indiscretions, and not repeat them anymore, and that is the message I would like to leave my audience.

If a New Age is to come, it must be good, and how would that be possible, if any part of the mess we've made of the world, and our individual lives, were included.

The Kennedys

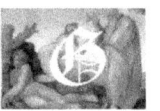 *iven the chance*
they would have changed
the world;
within them was a
power incredible,
that allowed them to be bold.

On podiums they would stand,
giving speeches that today we would judge
to be sermons.
Their quest was to do their best to relieve
mankind of its burdens.

Scholarly, they each were.
They knew how to give themselves an
inspirational spur.
When they were lost,
others realized what could have been
gained,
had they remained.

Memories of their acts, and words, can
brighten the sky,
which begs the question; why did they
have to die?

Leaders of their calibre were not to follow.
Their ideas others would borrow;
without giving credit to those
in whose footsteps they would follow.

With penetrating eyes

The Trinity Manifesto; Vol. I

they would survey a scene.
Distinguish so fast what needed to be
corrected;
others would wonder where the wrongs
had even been.

The Kennedy quest
was to always do their best.
All that they required,
they expected from themselves.
Was thiAfter all, solutions aren't provided
by elves.

Relentlessly they pursued their goals.
With diligence they treated their affairs.
Managed did they, to get things done,
despite occasionally accepting dares,
but never one that would involve a gun;
like all humans they needed a bit of fun.

The Trinity Manifesto; Vol. I

*Their vision was to make the world a
better place for us all.
Till this day we deeply mourn their fall.*

What Should A Jew Do?

 he Jew boy walks home,
from the Yeshiva, which is
his school.
The path is made of cobbled stone.
Many a rock from here he has thrown.

Fields and meadows lay each side.
The panorama is wide open.
Few places exist that can serve as a secure
place to hide.

Nearby, is the village where he resides;
a collection of shacks, huts, bungalows,
roads, and dirt paths, that serve as
carriage routes.
Here men, usually, don't bother to wear
suits.
They work as laborers.
Many must carry on their bent backs
heavy, burdensome, canvas sacks.

The women feed chickens, and goats,
sharing tales, stories, and Yiddish
jokes.
Their hands are often covered with grime,
and the smell of filthy, dirty, socks;
but when relatives and friends arrive to
share toasts,
they are the ones that serve as their loving
hosts.

The Trinity Manifesto; Vol. I

Each home is bordered with an old rickety
wooden fence.
In many a yard there is a special area,
where there is placed a comfortable,
beautiful, bench.

The men gather here to chat and talk,
Women and young girls serve traditional
dishes.
Each one is given his own special fork.

Don't base a judgment merely on how a
place looks;
much might appear to be in a state of
squalor.
So many here shout and holler;
but here is where many devote much time
to reading holy books.

The state one must live in,
says little about the depth of the
knowledge a person has within.
The willingness to learn and study hard,
can lead to a better understanding of the
time when all did begin.

The boy walks tall, with his chin held
high.
For all his life he has decided never to tell
a lie.
Truth is golden, and should be valued
above all else.
This is how we should measure the value
of ones' self.

The Trinity Manifesto; Vol. I

On his death bed, where he must muster
    his last sigh,
remembering he has always striven to be a
    good Jew,
with an open heart that reflects comfort
    and grace,
he will then express his love and devotion
    toward others;
then wish his dear ones a sincere goodbye.

The Torah and Talmud are held tightly in
    one hand.
The other sways with the greatest of ease.
He imagines a gentle caressing breeze,
as well as palm trees and soft sand.
One day he hopes he will be able to return
    to his Homeland.

Once he reaches the villages' central
    square,
he notices the stores are vacant, and
    empty;
the market stalls have been left bare.
All appears still, but nearby awaits a
    treacherous lair.
Several youngsters are waiting for him
    there,
hiding behind a rusty iron gate.
Their intent is to wait till he passes
then whips and chains will be used to give
    lashes.

Whistling a tune a Rabbi once taught him,
    he neglects to survey what is around.

The Trinity Manifesto; Vol. I

His mind is concerned with the coming
* Sabbath, when he will wear a shoal,*
* the sacred gown.*

Deprived of even a moment to prepare,
the troublesome youths appear as fast as a
* hare.*
They encircle, determined to cause a great
* deal of misery.*
Trapped, the Jew accepts he has been
* deprived of his liberty.*

What does a Jew do when he encounters
* the unknown?*
He waits to see what the other will
* demand;*
a gift, a way to punish, or maybe the help
* of a loan.*

Mocking, lecherous, voices ring out.
Disparaging words are caste to make him
* feel fear.*
Because he is a Jew, he does not.
The Lord protects him because He is near.

The books are drawn to his chest to offer
* protection.*
Because he is one among The Chosen,
he knows he is special by natural selection.
Few in number, each must fight to survive.
Due to this reason, till this day, they have
* managed to thrive.*
Many in the past, however, have been
* persecuted, and as a result died.*

The Trinity Manifesto; Vol. I

One after another, cruel names are used to
describe
his Faith, family, and himself; none of this
could possibly be true.
Evidence is present in family portraits and
trophies
that are above his home fireplace on a
mantle shelf.

Pain rips through his back, arms, and legs.
Suffering, experiencing great pain, he falls
to the ground.
So proud, not for a moment does he
consider to beg, or ask for mercy.

It seems an eternity before they end their
cruel game.
Many others have suffered the same degree
of humiliation;
throughout the ages things have remained
much the same.

Covered with red is his shirt from his nose
that is now swollen.
Evidence of the crime is clearly shown.
His love for justice and The Lord has
grown.

He brushes the dirt from his sleeves and
pants,
then gathers the pages dispersed from his
torn, broken, books.
Then an epiphany arrives all of a sudden,
all that matters is to have self-control, not
to be a glutton.

The Trinity Manifesto; Vol. I

Instilled in his heart is the love for others
    of the past.
Relatives, neighbors, friends, how they
    died;
to the lions and sea they have been caste.
The Chosen people must continue.
Above all else, this is their most important
    task.
Finally he approaches his family's home.
Here his Abba and Ema reside.
There he feels safe,
his sores will be covered,
and will be able to rest each weary bone.

Practically outside the small bungalow's
    front door,
once more a threat presents itself.
This time the enemy can possibly be
    defeated.
On top of the wooden gate his sole
    opponent is seated.
A punch is thrust, but misses,
as the other hand of the Jew bashes.
He can see now the degree of his pain.
For this reason, he feels quite sane.

The joke is at hand;
how did he ever think he had a chance?
So many peoples have become extinct.
The Hebrews till this day can enjoy the
    game of the dance.

Wailing the pitiful cries of a small child,
licking the wounds he deserves to get,
he races home, probably to cover his head,

The Trinity Manifesto; Vol. I

in the room where lies his bed.

Standing before both his parents,
after passing the threshold of his family's
    sanctuary,
Ema covers her child with hugs and kisses,
Abba watches weary and tired from the
    long day at the factory.

A bowl seeping steam, smelling of herb and
    spices,
is served to please his nose and gullet.
His father, meanwhile
gives him a sermon on the worth of a
    bullet.

"Always do what is right;
pleasing The Lord is the ultimate gift."
Abba preaches, while he strokes the boys
    shoulder.
We each in life must learn to grow bolder.

The calloused, cracked, and wrinkled, hand
    of the elder,
holds the chin of his son.
Struggles never cease, toils never end,
the lessons of life have just begun.

Pride fills the man's heart, and reddens his
    cheeks.
For so long he has waited for this moment,
seeming an eternity; actually, it has only
    been weeks.

Time passes so quickly, where does it go?

The Trinity Manifesto; Vol. I

*All his life he's wondered, wanted to
    know;
maybe one day, before he should pass
    away.*

*The end never seems possible.
He hoped he'd have a son,
who could share with him,
the joys, wonders, and terrors of this scary
    show.*

The Miracle of Life

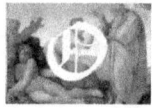

ne among many,
I walk and stumble,
along a gravel patched road.

A man falls by the wayside.
Each one looks the other way
as if he doesn't care.
Nothing could be further from the truth;
    The night has grown dark;
    men growl with despair
as they walk side by side as a pair.

to continue onward, along the tunnel of
    death,
is now the ultimate dare.

Men in black suits watch.
They strike with a cane.
Do they know, understand
the land and time from which they came?

Their orders that bark,
note that this is not possible;
how they now treat these men is damn
    horrible.

The Trinity Manifesto; Vol. I

Trembling, an old man falls to his knees.
A Nazi slams a rod into his face.
"Have mercy, dear God, stop, please!"
Is his cry given.
He now shudders with the pain that racks
  his bones.
His hatred stings like a swarm of bees.

"Stand, march, or face your end";
a sinister voice says to the now slain soul.
For months he has had to eat
from a stained, chipped, bowl.

"How can I when I have no strength left?"
"You have no choice; it is for your best."
With the last morsel of energy that
  remains,
the grandfather of many lifts his head.
Each movement helps toward his cause.
These are the sole things from which he
  gains.

Fearful that his demise is so very near,
he pulls himself up.
The thirst he now bares is incredibly acute.
It is not water he craves,
but the warmth of a thick, dark, beer.

Two steps more are taken,
then he collapses once more to the ground.
The Guard that hovers over
now appears as a sinister hound.

The Trinity Manifesto; Vol. I

The lips part and form a grin.
Why is this happening, the old man asks;
did I commit some heinous, terrible, sin?

Will he offer me more time?
His legs now hold the strength of sheer
    lace.
The pistol at his head,
reveals this is not the case.
Their eyes now meet,
each one stares at the others face.
One is cold; the other is covered with a
    disguise.
The wrinkled, aged, one, hides the degree
    of his despise.

"You are vermin;
correction,
mice among men.
Deserve you all to live in a pig's pen.
That is where you belong;
secluded, alone, a ghettoized den."

From behind,
another cries for the others safety.
"Give the man a chance!"
Once he reflects,
the elder enjoyed the gift of dance.

Suddenly, a boom sounds.
A bullet enters
the heart of the one that spoke.
In an instant, he has now fallen.

The Trinity Manifesto; Vol. I

Instead of a helpless lost soul;
a world now opens that is shiny, golden.
God Himself appears,
immeasurable beyond belief;
such is the magnitude of His scope.

Once his heart beats its last,
together, at once, he lies in peace.
Strange at this time
there should pass a family of geese.

Is this a symbol, sign?
Does it make up
for a life full of sweat, dirt, and grime?

The sight does not escape the
wise, elderly, fellow;
his cries of anguish and rage
are so loud they bellow.

To help mask how unsettled he feels
*   within,*
he digs deep into his shirt pocket for his
*   gin.*
Next he grabs the Jewish grandfather,
and carries him over to a soiled garbage
*   bin.*
He shoves within
the head of the one many have called a
*   Sage.*
The pistol is pressed against his forehead.
Is the Nazi's world now covered in a
*   haze?*

The Trinity Manifesto; Vol. I

*"Please, I beg of you, give me a chance to
    speak.*
*Am I not worthy of this, before you choose
    to end all my days?"*

"Say what you have to say, and fast!"
"Give me a bit of time,
they will, after all, be my last."

The Nazi remains silent
*while the grandfather formulates the
    words he wishes to utter.*
*"Why am I the one that deserves to live in
    a gutter?"*

Instead of an answer,
*blood is sent gushing from a gaping
    wound.*
All is over, a life has passed.
*The soldier is responsible for the others
    doom.*
What wasn't heard
was the silent wish for a miracle.

*Strange it is the Nazi soon dies from the
    shot of an arrow.*
*Was the prayer answered? We really
    don't know;*
*but who from the nearby hill held the
    strong bow*

Totalitarian regimes seek to totally rule a population through a "central body"; they dictate how people should speak, act, behave, cloth themselves, and so on and so forth; if final rulings are made by a single individual, the result is much the same. How was Hitler any worse than Stalin?

When people are allowed to decide for themselves how they wish to live their lives, while no justice system is in place – "inverted totalitarianism" – disorder, anarchy, chaos, and violence, will inevitably result.

Totalitarian regimes, and fascist dictators, create laws to justify their acts; people in Hyper-democratic societies, such as Canada, lie, deceive, cheat, and steal, to get whatever happens to their fancy at any particular time. When people are given a free hand to rule their own affairs, a brute will soon be the result.

In the novel "1984", George Orwell created the term "crimestop", which means essentially that the mind is unable to process certain data; the intent being that the perpetration of a crime be allowed to transpire without interruption – protective stupidity.

"Excuse me officer, I've just been mugged. He ran in this direction. Did you see him? He's about 6 foot tall, with dark, brown, hair."

"How may I be of assistance? You're out of breath, maybe you should take to take a seat, and rest."

"But officer…"

"Sorry, I can't help you; I just remembered a place I'm supposed to be."

Too often people decide to take the easy path, and become a member of a herd, reducing oneself to little more than a mindless automaton, rather than having the courage to stand up for what is right and just

 rotsky was a man
whom many think
did harm.
Red and white did clash,
but a change was needed in a dash.

Fairness, equality, a means to survive;
is what he wanted to arrive.
No longer relying on hash, or revelling in
cash.

People would flock to see him speak,
In awe they would be,
believing he held for them the key.
No longer did they want to live on a leash,
feeling they are nothing but a leech.

The Trinity Manifesto; Vol. I

Peering through those spectacles,
he saw a future spectacular.
By leading the way,
people would sleep on something better
*   than straw and hay.*

None of those things came to be,
because a man named Stalin made him flee.

To this day we should wonder;
how much a better place this could be,
if things had happened at the pace seen by
*   he?*
Maybe today we'd all be free!!

Martin Luther King

 artin Luther king, was a
man many thought
would bring them the
Rights they sought,
and needed to take away
memories of the times they were bought.
For pennies they could be sold,
and for this reason
found it so difficult to stand bold.
For all these things Martin earnestly
pleaded.

He saw a "promised land".
Take my hand, he said, and like a band of
brothers
we will find our way there,
and from the mountain top we'll stare,
and think how rich we are now.

Poverty was a thing of the past,
far off in the distance it lay.
Soon buried beneath the lies of men
who thought solely of themselves,
and said; "To hell with them!"

Like so many who strive for justice,
he was set down in his prime.
Murdered by the kind that should not exist
in man.

His presence was golden.

The Trinity Manifesto; Vol. I

His words rich in meaning.
He had all he needed.

Such strength.
A character so wise.
Young also.
It seems, like so many others,
because of this,
He died!

"Only the good die young."

The
Evil Doers

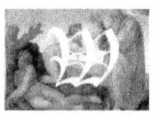 *hy do they wish to confuse?*
To cover the truth!

All those who deceive have the same
objective;
at any cost to another they will do as they
please.
Some decide they are evil, others, unwise.
Today they appear everywhere;
standing on a corner, sitting in an office,
or in a kitchen cooking fries.

Most are much the same.
They bear no consequence, experience no
guilt,
when their acts cause harm.
For those who have the courage to protest,
prisons have been built.

Those who are corrupt,
today hold the reins of power.
The path we follow,
is determined by them.

If others decide the ride is not to their
liking;
where is the chance to get off,
to find another path?

The Trinity Manifesto; Vol. I

None of these things exist today.
The bad believe they will last till the end.

Truth be told,
never will they arise again.
To hell, each one will go.

The good will rise,
and rejoice that by their side
is love, care, and plenty.
All the things they lacked on this earth.

They have been offered everlasting life;
a new birth!

A Good Person

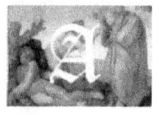 priest presents
a face that is kind to all.
"I offer you solace,
 a listening ear.
I will do my utmost to lessen your fear."

The person is unique;
created by a Church
that is simply a freak.

In the Vatican people pray;
offer words of guidance and hope,
while, really, men play with children,
because they are gay.

The outside is astonishing;
great works of art, spirals soar into the
        sky,
paintings describe scenes from The Bible;
words of truth,
however, about their deeds
would be considered libel.

"I stand before you as a man of God.
He speaks to me, I can speak to you",
absurd you may think,
the combination of the two.

Ridiculous sermons, venomous deeds.

The Trinity Manifesto; Vol. I

A persona is a façade;
it hides a disquieting reality.
Protection is derived from the essential
  faculty.

Often that which is soft,
is, in fact, hard.
Extremely difficult it is to face;
things in accordance with how they are.

The most suspicious character
is often a charming Barrister.
"Justice is what we seek", proudly he will
  state his case.
Conviction will be accomplished
through a Legal System that is brute force.

Little of what we actually see,
is how we would like it to be.
Dark is light.
Light is faint.

Observing the Artist as he struggles to
  paint;
there is an honest man, baring his soul for
  all to see.
Kind to others when away from his work,
but, harsh to those who present an obstacle
  before his goal;
to know Him who resides in his soul

Leon Trotsky

Life is not an easy matter...
You cannot live through it without falling into frustration and
cynicism unless you have before you a great idea which raises you
above personal misery, above weakness, above all kinds of perfidy
and baseness.

The depth and strength of human character are defined by its moral
reserves. People reveal themselves completely only when they are
thrown out of the customary conditions of their life, for only then do
they have to fall back on their reserves.

Benjamin Franklin

Money has never made man happy, nor will it, there is nothing in its
nature to produce happiness. The more of it one has the more one
wants.

It is the working man who is a happy man. It is the idle man who is
a miserable man.

Who is wise? He that learns from everyone. Who is powerful? He
that governs his passions. Who is rich? He that is content. Who is
that? Nobody

Ramakrishna Paramahamsa

God is in all men, but not all men are in God; that is why we suffer.

Bondage is of the mind; freedom too is the mind. If you say, "I am a
free soul. I am a son of God who can blind me", free you shall be.

A man once asked Sigmund Freud; what makes you better than other people? Answer:...because I can honestly say, I have never intentionally harmed another person in my entire life.

The children are our future!

If we are prepared to acknowledge the shortcomings in the education system today, there's no reason why the future can't be bright for each and every one of us, I say.

The essential component that will allow this to transpire is a renewed appreciation for greatness, and making sure nutrients are available for such an individual's fullest potential to be actualized.

Many of the world's problems have been left unattended for so long, only men of Einstein's caliber are going to get us out of the pit we've dug for ourselves, and find a path to the heavens where our spirits belong.

"Love Is the Nature of Existence" is available on Amazon, and bookstores everywhere.

The Creator

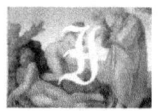

mmersed within Myself,
I see visions from beyond.
A kaleidoscope of colours hides among the
fringe;
all of Me is there, to Me I bring.

The angels speak many voices, many
tongues,
they fill the Universe, that am I.
Like a desert from Heavenly Mother,
there on the shelf is a delicious pie.

A feast it is to know I have so much to
relish.
All is as it should be,
nowhere is there a single blemish.

Goodness is a word, vibrating throughout.
Few know, have any conception, what I
am about.

Never ending, fascinating, mesmerizing,
features.
A movie of actors, stages, curtains, plays;
throughout eternity, this is time,
a new one I enjoy each of My days.

The Trinity Manifesto; Vol. I

To those not yet in My presence, they
    appear as if murky,
distinguished as if somewhat a haze.

Illusions create this perception.
It is neither true nor reality;
they still have not developed
the essential faculty.

To realize fullness in all its goodness,
offered are treasures containing
    innumerable fruits;
each one delicious, juices of wine,
    succulent,
served on dishes of silver that are fine;
hardly a pair of dirty, grimy, smelly, boots.

All that dazzles the eye, tingles the senses,
    heightens awareness,
is that which is Me.
From a distant island a Port awaits,
offering safe harbour to those lost at sea.

Rocky waves, reptilian creatures, swift
    currents that carry you away;
fear none of these,
you are here by My side;
listen loved ones to these words I say.

My wish is for all to experience peace,
    tranquillity, security of mind.
The presence of a roaring lion, mighty bear,
should not create a shudder, any pain;

The Trinity Manifesto; Vol. I

they are a part of Me, being of the utmost
* kind.*

I wish for no one to suffer,
but my riches can be desired for no other
* way.*
Without sadness, how can you experience
* joy?*
This is not a game to me, I see no one as a
* toy.*

I hold each enveloped in My sanctified
* cocoon.*
How dearly do I love thee.
I seek not to scare, frighten, or confuse.

Watch the mission that is carried by a bee.
I must defend all that I represent.
Stings that ignite furious storms,
repel the unjust, wicked, and impure.
Lessons are told in each tone that scolds.

Michelangelo near broke his back making a
* miraculous masterpiece.*
In every way possible I will do My utmost
to insure the dark, as a force, will cease,
then I relinquish My quest,
it is over, complete,
now you and I will have peace.

Historical Idiocy

 he Jews, it is said, did the worst thing of all;
they deprived us of a man
that stands above us all.
He is seen, quite literally, as being that
     tall.

The contradiction is clearly apparent,
the man was a Jew,
heaven sent.

How far does man think things through?
Frankly, presently, I haven't a single clue;
thus, nights can be long, garnering
     throughout little, if any, sleep,
waiting we might, for the sound of a
     sinister clown;
it could be a shout, a screech, a scream,
or merely, a creepy, haunting, boo.

The darkest time never fled mankind.
Hideous butchery, slavery, and so much
     more,
has taken place for ever so long;
many consider it somewhat a bore.

The diversity, varieties, present in man,
give us the kindling to fire imaginations.

The Trinity Manifesto; Vol. I

Never should we allow populations
to become as ashes;
their souls, essence, leave us as twirling
    clouds,
moving upward through the sky.

The air present around us is a treasure,
beyond which none can compare.
It is hatred, ignorance, malicious
    indifference,
that has darkened
man, child, earth, moon, women, and the
    wild,
that leaves us wading in horrid pools of
    indifference and despair.

Please let us all hope that one day
    harmony will arise,
all then will be enabled to be as one.
Beaut, and grace, celestial visions,
shall be seen within even the fluttering
    wings of those we call flies.

How shall this have a possibility, a chance
    to come about?
Clues, indications, signs and symbols, have
    been left in our collective past.

Study, examine, research books,
letters, songs, and poems,
given by the Great Ones that have already
    been;
then, without a shadow of a doubt, man
    will last and last and last;

not, God damn it, on some distant planet.
The chance to put things right is singular.

No longer shall we procrastinate.
Each day provides the splendours and
    treasures that fuel minds,
and provide us with the answers we so
    desperately need.

Are they, as once was, the Jews?
In a sense, of course!
We are, one race, one people, so alike.
If we choose,
tomorrow we could place ourselves on the
    right path,
then, just like riding a bike, never could we
    forget, or unlearn,
allow ourselves to hurt or burn.

Finally, as one,
we will realize we have become our best.
Pleasure supreme, bliss evermore, will be
    realized,
and so we will be given our earnest rest;
call it heaven, paradise, samadhi, nirvana;
what could any of it possibly matter?

These are just man made words;
poetical in nature, strange, a variety of
    meanings,
so many, a man can lose sense of what he
    can be sure.
Count them, possibly, on the wings of
    those we refer to simply as birds.

The Trinity Manifesto; Vol. I

Who can describe the unknown, that
  which has not been seen?
Life is a mystery, the greatest of all;
so much encompasses, involves, and lies
  between.
Left we can be breathless, and sink to our
  knees.
Don't feel you ever have the right to stand
  on another mans' feet;
look upon yourself always as being
  complete.

Now, in the past, whenever that may have
  been,
in the future, far in the distance, forever
  more,
paradise is here with us now;
not on some long forgotten and distant
  obscure shore.

Often, it has been believed by many that
the Indians knew of these things;
as a greeting they often
say; How!

Life can be, should be, oh so simple.
Doesn't that make you smile?
Look inside, sentinel being,
open your eyes;
on each side there is a dimple!

Day 4

Paul McCartney
Yesterday

Yesterday all my troubles seemed so far away
Now it looks as though they're here to stay
Oh I believe in yesterday
Suddenly I'm not half the man I used to be
There's a shadow hanging over me
Oh yesterday came suddenly
Why she had to go I don't know
She wouldn't say
I said something wrong, now I long for yesterday
Yesterday, love was such an easy game to play
Now I need a place to hide away
Oh I believe in yesterday

A LETTER TO GOD

We are all the children of the universe.
We will live in a world beyond war.
We will live in a world beyond greed and starvation.
We will live in a world of peace, love, and understanding.
Because we are the children of the universe.

Jon Anderson/Indigenous Journey

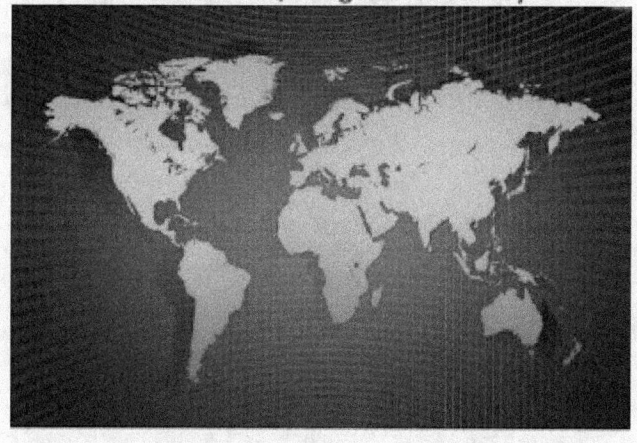

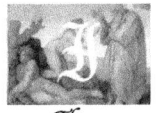 stood there watching clouds,
      hovering, suspended, in space.
The near as distant as the far.

The planets hadn't yet arrived,
so the Sun was my beacon of hope.
My Father spoke,
then a world awakened.
I was amazed by the beauty now held within my eye.

I looked down below,
And saw a planet I wished to know.
Upon my chariot I skimmed the dimensions of limitless space,
And eventually, before I knew it,
Arrived at a place I could call home.

The deepest secrets I knew before,
collapsed within my being,
So I wouldn't know, or understand,
what it was I was seeing.

The Trinity Manifesto; Vol. I

Dark became light, light became dark,
and the people that surrounded me,
inhabited the shades that lie in-between.

A day arrived when I left for school;
afraid, because others now saw me as a fool;
someone who was merely a toy
to keep them amused.
For many days forth
words were used with the intent to abuse.

The fields were full, lush, and green.
Rivers chuckled over rocks,
while bubbles echoed over swaying streams,
as I stared up at the night sky,
and witnessed the bright glow of a radiant moon.

Where is it I now belong?
The chariot that took me here was now gone.

The days, weeks, and months, passed,
while I learned more about the ways of the world,
and the nature of the beauty that encompassed me.

The people in my midst seemed entirely unacquainted
with the magic, and wonder, that abounds;
enclosed in measures that should simply astound.

Silently I stood,
watching these creatures who appeared not at all like me;
their days wasted,
while performing dastardly deeds
so callously and carefree.

The Trinity Manifesto; Vol. I

My mind searched the realm of angels,
trumpets, harps, and song.
It was only for these things I could long.

The building I would call home
was situated in different places.
No matter where,
I explored outward, and within,
while avoiding those who danced
on the shoes of others,
obviously not in harmony with
the domain tranquilly contained within me.

More years passed,
and I grew familiar with the extent
people squandered their time on this earth,
and thought it best
to despise the wisdom I'd obtained,
although I already knew it
while in the clouds from which I came.
But my spirit could not stay here;
the heavens drew it to herself,
and I quietly again hid among stars;
silently waiting till my chariot took me down below.

What had happened, my dear God!
No more were there shades of grey.
Many had acquired a brute nature,
that now found humour in death,
and relished the opportunity
to squeeze life out of matter.

My identity was now transparent,
because people were transparent to me.

The Trinity Manifesto; Vol. I

My worth was measured in objects I left behind,
not the knowledge contained in my mind,
that could make men free.

My life became a travelling show;
I, a bumper car;
others would crash into
while hollering wails of laughter;
Exhibiting the extent they are
glum, moody, sad, and filled with despair;
with lives they sought to fill with the objects that fell,
as I was jostled side to side, here and there,
till my cupboards were empty,
and left completely bare.

For a time this continued,
until I realized this is all I have left;
a circus fairground filled with clowns who are ghouls,
performing acrobatic displays
in an attempt to entertain;
all the while I could only stare,
and wonder where on earth they came.

What could I do?
Where could I go?
Why, in heaven's name, was I put here?
Only once I understood the extent
of the state of these affairs,
did I discover my true calling.

Everything was out of control,
and I was brought here to show
the way to make things straight;
by reminding people of principles

The Trinity Manifesto; Vol. I

belonging to the thoughts present in the beginning;
remembering the days of old,
so the world could once again become anew.

Eons ago I stood among clouds, surveying from a mountaintop
the stars before, behind, and above,
thinking how wonderful is the
word we call
Love.

Alan Parson's Project/Time

Time, flowing like a river. Time, beckoning me
Who knows where we shall meet again
If ever
But time
Keeps flowing like a river
To the sea

Goodbye my love
Maybe forever
Goodbye my love,
The tide waits for me
Who knows where we shall meet again
If ever
But time
Keeps flowing like a river (on and on)
To the sea, to the sea

Albert Einstein

The only reason for time is so everything doesn't happen at once
Any intelligent fool can make things bigger and more complex... It
takes a touch of genius...and a lot of courage to move in the opposite
direction"

Carl Gustav Jung

The dream is the small hidden door in the deepest most intimate
sanctum of the soul, which opens to the primeval cosmic night that
was the soul long before there was conscious ego and the will to be
soul far beyound what a conscious ego could ever reach.

JOHN LENNON
Working Class Hero

As soon as you're born they make you feel small
By giving you no time instead of it all
Till the pain is so big you feel nothing at all
A working class hero is something to be

Keep you doped with religion and sex and T.V.
And you think you're so clever and classless and free
But you're still fucking peasants as far as I can see
A working class hero is something to be

I Am the Walrus

I am he, as you are he, as you are me, and we are all together.
See how they run, like pigs from a gun, see how they fly,
I'm crying.

Sitting on a cornflake, waiting for the van to come.
Corporation tee-shirt, stupid bloody Tuesday.
Man, you been a naughty boy, you let your hair grow long.
I am the eggman, they are the eggmen.
I am the Walrus, goo goo g'joob

Woman is a Nigger of the World

We make her paint her face and dance
If she won't be a slave, we say that she don't love us
If she's real, we say she's trying to be a man
While putting her down, we pretend that she's above us

And did those feet in ancient time
Walk upon England's mountain green?
And was the holy lamb of God
On England's pleasant pastures seen?

And did the Continence Divine
Shine forth upon our Clouded hills?
And was Jerusalem builded here
Among these dark satanic mills?

Bring me my bow of burning gold!
Bring me my arrows of desire!
Bring me my spear! Oh clouds, unfold!
Bring me my chariot of fire!

I will not cease from mental fight.
Nor shall my sword sleep in my hand,
Till we have built Jerusalem
In England's green and pleasant land.

(William Blake)

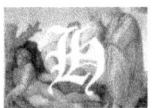 e had hair that flowed,
in every direction it would go.
He laughed, he cried, he played the violin,
he could also view the universe
in a way no man before could have foreseen.

Where do men such as he come from?
His gifts were plentiful.
He strove to reach his full potential;
surely, this goal stands for us all.

Look into his eyes; they sparkle; the stars lie there.
This is what makes us stare; but the question is still there:
why do other men keep their minds so bare?

Try, we should, to be like him; striving to always learn:
don't treat this as if it is some dare.

It is your choice; you can remain as you are;
work hard, though, and one day your thoughts
will flow with the speed of a hare.

One day, I hope, we'll all arrive there;
realize first, that to start,
you will need a heart.

Jung

 ung was kind.
Not wanting us to be blind,
he taught us to be kind to the young.

During youth we develop as a person.
Be careful with those during this time,
otherwise with a sentence
they will be dealt to prison.

There are many parts to man, Jung knew;
also parts unseen.
Some,
if you are careful, you will gradually know,
while others are mysterious,
and appear merely as a show.

To explore this stage that lies beneath the floor,
we need first to find some door to get there.
We need to follow each stair;
be careful, though,
it can be scary down there.

What may lurk in the shadows can cause a
scare,
but, throughout it all, we shouldn't have a care;
it is not as if there lies a bear down there.

Though, at first, there is darkness,
our eyes acclimatize,
then we see it all, we are just plain kindness.

The deeper you go,
closer to the surface we
arrive.

THE
COLLECTIVE
UNCONSCIOUS

Carl Gustav Jung has the unique distinction of being the creator of the term, "collective unconscious"; which happens to represent the same as what I call within "Love Is the Nature of Existence"; The Source, the well-spring of life, The Grand Animator, The Lord, among other expressions; most, however, are predisposed to simply use the word, "God".

Depth Psychology could be described as an attempt to understand the nature of God; most are far more comfortable with the label, "religion", as a way of defining such an undertaking

Carl Jung envisioned the mind of Man as consisting of compartments. What we are aware of he called the "conscious mind"; what we have access to, but are not typically aware of, he called the "pre-conscious mind", In order to better comprehend the implication; picture yourself sitting in a chair in your living room, looking around and becoming aware of the furnishings and ornaments within, and while doing so remembering a lamp you stored some while ago in a closet adjacent to the room, that would require a few steps and the opening of a door to retrieve.

We also have an "unconscious mind"; what this signifies, (equating the mind to a house we reside within), is that there is a cellar in the basement we don't know about, and stored within are things that belong to us that we are not aware of; say a crystal chandelier you inherited that a relative placed it in the room and

143

neglected to tell you about; therefore, both the cellar and the chandelier belong to you, but you have yet to be informed of such being the case.

The "collective unconscious", unlike the other components that make up our personality, is common, and identical, within each of us, and cannot be contained in any manner. There are, however, "elements", "key ingredients", that formulate the nature of the "collective unconscious"; Carl Jung called these, "archetypes"; to make an analogy, in order to better illustrate the nature of what I've detailed, picture the "collective unconscious" as actually being a self-contained unit of some sort, maybe a house, and if someone were asked to describe the elements that make up this house, one would probably automatically respond by mentioning such things as a roof, door, windows, etc., etc..

The primary purpose of religion since the dawn of human civilization has been to better understand the archetypes; mythology, and symbols, have been the primary instruments used to achieve this objective, and the finest examples can be found in what we commonly refer to as "holy scriptures". A "myth", therefore, can be used as a means to relay information about the nature of a window of the house that belongs to each and every one of us. Novels can be used for the same purpose; the plot is used to familiarize the reader with characters.

Carl Jung explains that the manner in which we can better understand our nature, to realize ourselves, to achieve "Self-realization", is by a process of "individuation"; although we all stem from the same ocean, in a manner of speaking, we are all unique as individuals, and by acquiring an understanding of the individual parts that make up who we are, we actually, at the same time, learn about the connection we have with every other person in this world; that is why the U.S. Constitution describes all men as being created equal, and democracy, as it's detailed in the U.S. Bill of Rights, insures we have the freedom to discover our individuality.

To make an analogy, picture yourself as a lake; the water that constitutes the lake comes from a river which is connected to an ocean. The lake, however, is quite different from the ocean, and the type of life forms that exist in the lake are different from those in the ocean; which is controlled by such factors as the temperature of the water, how the temperature varies throughout the year, the depth of the water, the forms of vegetation within, and so on and so forth.

All the water, or energy, to make another analogy, that makes us who we are, comes from the ocean, The Source, The Lord, God, the "collective unconscious", and, therefore, ordinarily we are entirely unaware of our true nature.

The energy that seeps into the conscious mind stems from innate qualities common within each of us; the "instincts"; they oppose one another, and, as a result, create a balance; yin, yang, dark, light, destructive, constructive, love and death.

Thoughts and ideas are formulated by the use of these forms of energy that represent our emotions; therefore, one can conclude that people never actually consciously decide any action; we only seek to understand something once it has already occurred; to make an analogy, fuel is placed in the tank of your car, the car is then able to travel a certain distance. Once the tank is empty you find yourself at a country Inn, and you believe you decided to visit this place for a short vacation. This may have been the reason why there was such an amount of fuel in the tank, but the important part to remember is that you didn't consciously decide how much fuel was placed in the tank.

There, in a nut shell, is depth psychology described using Jungian terminology, and if one religiously utilizes the ingredients that constitute its making, one can say that he is practicing a religion; he is attempting to reach, fully realize, the "collective unconscious". In the "East" the word "yogi" is used to describe such a person, and he said to practice "yoga"; the word means, "to yoke", join - man to God, the conscious mind with the collective unconscious; the lake with the ocean.

The dreadful thing about Man is that instead of using this wonderful, tremendous, knowledge to better himself, he decided instead to use it as a means to control and exploit others.

There are presently many dangerous elements that have been deliberately incorporated into our environment, and because of our lack of knowledge, and awareness, they have entered our lives, and made us something other than what we are supposed to be; not a human being, but a brute.

The best protection a person can have is the ability to think, reason, decipher, and discern; this is much the same as having the ability to look through a window at the air outside, and if you think it's safe to breath, you open the window; maybe, due to being cautious, just a bit at first. The person devoid of the ability to be analytic is much the same as not having a plain of glass to serve as a boundary between you and the potentially toxic air outside.

Consider the following to exemplify my argument; the pentagram, (five pointed star encased in circle), within the Wicca religion, otherwise called Witchcraft, is used to represent the elements, earth, air, fire, and water, and the upward point is representative of the spirit; all these things contribute to life and are a part of each of us. Those that profess to practice Satanism, reverse the pentagram, and have it point downward, representative of their worship of things that destroy and degrade life. The Nazis perverted an ancient Sanskrit symbol representative of cosmic unity by reversing the direction the angles.

I've just provided two examples of symbols being used to distance people from reality, and persuade them to do something contrary to what they think they are doing.

There is actually no such thing as black magic, or black masses, in the Wiccan religion; the commonly accepted creed for this form of "psychology" is:

"If it harms none; do what thou will".

At no other time in history did man reveal his capacity to destroy, and cause suffering, than during the Second World War. At the same time bonfires fueled by books written by some of the greatest minds ever were watched as a spectacle by the masses.

This act was not pardoned, forgiven, or forgotten; history has shown that we have taken ourselves as a consequence to the brink of self-annihilation. Surely, by now, we have learned our lesson, and The Lord will provide us our saving grace once again - the Jews.

Credo

**Words inspired by the life of
Robert F. Kennedy**

The only chance we have of surviving as a species is by remembering our humanity; that our fellow man is also our brother, and we must care for each other as much as we care for ourselves; only then will the divine reach the Earth; after all, we are in fact spirit not matter, and there is nothing we cannot overcome if we determine to do so.

Day 5

The
Making

Who Made Me?

When I think of the story of my life, I realize the most important ingredients are provided in the beginning. I've been blessed to have lived a life populated with people from a diverse assortment of backgrounds.

The first place I lived was a town called Reading, in Britain, but the city of Liverpool seemed more my home, due to the people who enriched my life there in so many ways.

Some of my fondest memories took place in a clothing store, for example, where relations on my father's side would congregate. The air was usually stuffy and dusty, but the smiles, hellos, handshakes, and the occasional shilling quickly tucked in a back pocket, could brighten the gloomiest rainy day. My grandmother, Rose, and her sister, Jessie, would sit here often, chatting, while enjoying a cup of tea. I remember the pleasure of greeting an uncle who always had cheeks coloured a rosy red, whether he had a smile on his face or not; these were the kind of people I never grew bored being around; listening to their stories, and acknowledging how much they valued my presence. It has been gestures of kindness that have stuck with me to this day, reminding me of the goodness so many are willing to openly display.

A while later I moved to a village called Silverstone, but I was usually far more captivated by my trips to visit my father's relations in Liverpool, as well as my travels nearby to see my mother's friends, her brother, Graham, and his wife, among others; plus a lady with the last name, Mermaid, who led the Boy-scouts I was a member of. These are the experiences that have left the greatest impressions on my mind.

Even when I moved to Canada, to the city of Toronto, and attended a primary-school called, Dublin, my heart and soul remained in England, which I consider, to this day, to be my home.

My growth as a person has not been so much due to the books I've read, or the places I've been, but rather the people I've met, and had to privilege to have known; to be able to witness acts of kindness, has taught me what it means to be a part of humanity.

The names of the people who have left a meaningful mark on my life are so long, I could barely remember even a small portion. Many I know have passed away, but, I hope, wherever they may be, they are aware of how much they mean to me, and realize how much they helped me become me.

Who Made You?

any years ago, when I was just entering my teens, I acquired a puppy, a mixture of a basset hound and a dachshund, that I decided to name McDougal; apparently, according to my father, who provided the name, this shaggy haired pup, with enormous ears that flopped when he strutted around, reminded him of a gentleman with the same name he once knew whom he found in a similar manner "peculiar".

I was barely cognizant of the fact at the time, indeed for many years to follow, but, from this dog I acquired an understanding of what it means to human, which necessitates, as far as I am concerned; acquiring the capacity to love, being loyal, and learning the value of self-sacrifice. McDougal was able to practice these things, due to not having the handicap so many among the "human " species are burdened with; if I can make a blanket statement; without exception all the difficulties, burdens, hardships, misery, despair, and suffering, Man experiences, is due to his acquisition of an Ego. The simplest way I can think of to describe this term, is to label Man as being selfish; concerned with himself, or defending his self.

The word, "Love", to me means the opposite of all the terms used above. Love, in the regard most understand the word, means to feel affection for; contrary to popular belief, this does not mean how a person makes you feel, rather the manner in which you affect another, which then has an effect on you. In other words, a connection is made between two people that, in some capacity, is nourishing.

To give an example; say, I have a friend that is learning to play the piano, and I decide to buy a few scores of music that I present to him as a gift. The recipient then feels pleasure because the undertaking he has placed upon himself has been acknowledged by another, and the continuation of his growth as a musical artist will be facilitated by the practice of the music he has been provided. In return the person who presented the gift, is rewarded by acquiring an understanding of another person, and, also, hopefully, most likely at some point in the future, quality music to appreciate, and has the comfort of knowing he has sustained a career, delivering security to another person, both long term and short term.

One way of picturing what I have expounded is as follows; one person turns on a light so another can study better, in turn when the other goes to bed, the student turns off the light so he can sleep better.

This seems to be such a simple exchange that we should all learn to execute at an early age due to the obvious benefits involved, but what practically all of us can acknowledge very early in our lives is that most of those who comprise what we distinguish as the "human species", find it difficult to execute such forms of behaviour; despite the obvious rewards garnered by doing so; why should this be the case?

Allow me to answer this question by creating a scene in a forest involving two men walking side by side along a dirt path.

Both men walk at the same pace for a considerable distance, until they begin to feel fatigue due to the strain of walking so long; then, all of a sudden, one stumbles; collapsing on the man beside him, who then abruptly falls, head first, into the trunk of a tree. An unfortunate turn of events, one might imagine, but also recognizable as an inevitable possibility due to both becoming tired due to the stretch of time they've been walking.

They perceive each other as being a friend, therefore, one would probably most likely assume that if neither has been seriously injured, no great harm has been done, and they might decide it would be best to take a bit of a break before continuing their trek. If each properly acknowledges the nature of the circumstance, (rather than perceiving the event as an unfortunate incident), it can be viewed as a positive learning experience; by taking a break they are more likely not to encounter a similar incident in the future. It is essential to always heed one's limitations. The interpretation of any event is formulated on the basis of what one conceives has been derived from the experience.

Let me now begin the scenario I created before once again, but with one added ingredient – "ego", with a capital E – "Ego"; that which creates "suffering"; in the Buddhist sense.

The one that collides with the tree, resulting in a bonk on the head, turns to his partner, already labelled a "friend", and says; "That really hurt; aren't you going to apologize?"

His friend replies; "I didn't do it intentionally. I think my foot caught on something, which made me stumble into you."

"Well that's all well and good, but I want a formal apology, before I even think of continuing to walk with you!"

"I didn't do it on purpose, but if it will make you feel better; I apologize. Are we O.K. now?"

"I guess so"; his friend answers.

To take this scenario to the furthest degree in order to illustrate the extent to which "Ego" can cause a separation between people, (Love, on the other hand, is the opposite, it represents connectedness), the following will be used as an example.

The man, who received an injury by falling into a tree, and insisted on being given an apology, decides to allow his companion to walk ahead of him, instead of beside. He waits till they enter an area of heavy foliage, where he believes no one is around to see or hear them, then extracts a knife from the inside pocket of his jacket he is wearing, and lunges forward with the blade in his hand, resulting in a deep, penetrating, wound, causing his companion to fall to the ground, and quickly thereafter dying due to a loss of blood.

The victor, the murderer, waits till he is certain the man now lying on the forest floor is dead, and then wipes the blood from his knife with a few leaves plucked from a nearby branch.

Once he is sure it is clean, he takes a quick glance around to be sure no one could have witnessed the murder he has just committed. He then steps over the body of the person he once considered a friend, and continues to walk along the path at an even pace so as not to attract attention, or cause suspicion.

How is this possible? One might ask. The addition of just one variable to the scene, created an outcome so catastrophic, and definitely the opposite of what transpired when it was not included.

Ego, as I explained the term before, is a concern, or interest, in one's self. The self could be viewed as an object you consider valuable, and precious, which you keep locked in a glass case so it will be kept safe and secure, and you can also derive pleasure from having the opportunity to view it.

The man asking for an apology within the context provided could be considered as seeking a means to reacquire a sense of equilibrium, to establish a sense of security that has been compromised by the unexpected turn of events. This state could be considered as being comprised of primarily two elements; 1) doubt, and; 2) fear.

He might doubt the intention of his friend, and whether the apology is sincere; such being the case, he loses trust that his "friend" is someone he should feel secure around. These ideas, feelings, sensations, are, comparatively speaking, quickly formulated, and lead to a different perception and interpretation, of the events that have transpired.

It is quite possible in such a case, that there have been prior instances when he perceived someone as being honest, truthful, and, therefore, trustworthy, only to later discover that this assessment was entirely inaccurate. Following is an example of an instance that could have such an effect on a person.

Two men form a relationship, and believe they have a common interest in films after viewing one together on a computer; they then agree to meet to share the experience of watching a movie again. They convene at a coffee shop, and not long after, the one possessing the computer excuses himself to go to the bathroom, all the while looking forward to sharing opinions about a movie with someone bearing similar interests.

When he returns to the table where he'd been seated with the fellow "movie lover", he discovers he is no longer there, and his computer is nowhere in sight. In legal terms what has transpired is, "Fraud", the criminal act, however, is actually 'Theft". The word, fraud, merely describes the manner in which the act has taken place.

In other words, deception is being used to obtain objects, instead of, for example, someone pointing a gun at you, and insisting valuables be handed over · or else! This person, quite obviously, is not your friend, rather someone openly stating his intent and motive.

A "spy" is someone who uses fraud in order to obtain something he considers of value; "information". What harm could there possibly be, one would think, in telling someone you have "learned" to trust, where you were born, the schools you attended, even the bank where you have an account. The person is willingly handing over something the other party wishes to deprive you of; no force, or weapon, is needed. In the case of the two "movie lovers", if no one witnesses the perpetrator leaving with the computer, he can call his victim later and say the following;

"I got a call from a friend. He's in hospital. I had to leave right away. I didn't have the opportunity to tell you because you were in the bathroom, (the victim then provides the news)...You're computer's stolen! Oh my

God! What is the world coming to!? I'm so sorry. Would you like to meet for a coffee tomorrow, and we can maybe decide on a movie we can see together in a cinema.

The two men were never actually joined, or connected, therefore, one cannot, and will not, be affected by the hardship befallen on the other party due to his actions, and will only feel insecure, afraid, if there is a sense he's been caught in the act.

Practically everybody these days, most unfortunately, (whether or not they can conceive of the means used), has succumbed to utilizing different forms of fraud in order to obtain materials they are not entitled to. Another motive for committing fraud is so a person has the opportunity to repeat the act again, as opposed to someone who, to give an example, pulls a bank heist, and gets away with so much cash, he never expects to have to commit a criminal act again in order to obtain the lifestyle he wishes for himself.

The simple, and sad, truth, is that due to an evolutionary process people have, through various means, become disconnected from their fellow man, and as a consequence, do not love, but are instead consumed by the toll of continually attending to their own egos.

One can conclude, therefore, on the basis of the configuration of the elements I have illustrated, that evil, (the opposite of love), can be due, or created, by two factors; 1) an accumulation of doubt, fear, insecurity, and disconnectedness, as well as; 2) a lack of a conscience, or superego; one is not affected by the harm caused by his or her actions.

What this amounts to, generally speaking, is "ignorance", (acquired from the practice of continually ignoring things), and, therefore, the lesson is to learn from mistakes, errors in judgement, that adversely affect something outside of the self – that is why evil is sometimes labelled as being fraud, and is also described as "banal", and why we have the expression, "a wolf in sheep's clothing".

In our day to day affairs we all, one way or another, encounter examples of people displaying these traits, which explains why something that apparently, on the surface, appears superficial can, in a manner of speaking, escalate in the degree of its seriousness very quickly. I'll provide an incident that happened to me one morning in a bank as an example; to an outsider, the chain of events might appear chaotic, confusing, awkward, and maybe because of this, many might claim it really isn't important, and deserves to be brushed off one's shoulders – people just being people, in other words.

Man has never claimed, as far as I am aware, to be a rational animal throughout recorded history; I, on the other hand, believe all forms of human behaviour, small and large, have a reason, and a definite cause; in other words, contrary to the popular conception that we all make mistakes, our actions are rather the consequence of a number of "ingredients" that continue to induce an action; therefore, we may not consciously propose something to happen, but within our unconscious mind, we did intend the action to take place.

One way of viewing my argument is as follows; man (A) stumbles into man (B), causing him to hit his head on the trunk of a tree; man (B) then claims this was done intentionally. Man (A) refutes this assertion declaring that it wasn't intentional, but rather due to him being distracted; he wasn't watching carefully enough what lay before him on the path. If he, however, acknowledges responsibility, and has an earnest interest in making sure he doesn't do the same thing again, he will, no doubt, recognize that by being more aware of his surroundings, he can avoid repeating the same series of events. I will now relate the matter described above to the episode I mentioned that occurred in a bank.

Once entering a bank I approached the information desk/receptionist, and presented some papers, and declared that when I entered a bank account number on the internet, I was told it was "invalid". I also informed the young woman, (who was most likely in her early twenties), that I had previously purchased a pre-paid travel card, and encountered the same problem; but I had since discovered the cause – believing this information might offer assistance in determining why the same circumstance had arisen with the account in question.

What followed was a "muddled confusion" of responses, along with peculiar gestures directed toward the documents I'd presented, that made absolutely no sense, and, in fact, clearly contradicted what the "seeing eye" knew could in no way be correct. Suddenly I had a "eureka moment", and openly declared the truth; "I know what the problem is; you don't understand what the word "invalid" means...do you!?"

She then completely ignored what I had noted; so I repeated the question using different wording, and in a softer tone of voice, so as not to cause, to the best of my ability, embarrassment, while also eager to resolve the issue that brought me to the bank in the first place;

"Do you know the meaning of the word "invalid"?"

She swiftly exclaimed, "Yeh, I do!" While not even daring to look me in the eyes, but instead searching an area in the distance, off to one side, as if a heavenly body would miraculously materialize, and provide her the means to get out of the now awkward situation.

Then, without giving any hint as to her motive, she rose from her chair, and began circulating the desk, mumbling, "I'm getting someone else". I moved over one step, and said, using a higher volume of voice than before; "All I asked was whether you understood the meaning of the word invalid."

She walked about ten yards away, until the manager emerged from his office, and approached the desk, and asked; "How can I help you?"

"I'd like to know why she doesn't understand the word "invalid"; do you?"

"Why don't we deal with this matter in my office."

Before proceeding I said; "Before I do so, I should tell you that the word means; illegitimate, illegal". As I passed the desk I mentioned; "As a suggestion I recommend a dictionary be placed here", while tapping on the edge of the counter.

I was then told by the manager that the problem was caused by my tone of voice, and if I continued to use such a tone, he would close my bank accounts.

I believe most would consider his response to be an over-reaction, excessive, and quite unnecessary; but here is an insight as to why he used the words he did; he also declared; "I've dealt with you before, and I don't like the way you talk to my employees"; apparently, according to his judgment, I demean them!

"Excuse me! All I did was speak the truth. If they can't handle the truth, that's not my problem."

All he could claim following this point I'd made was; "Your tone of voice was the problem."

I again refuted this absurd insinuation by stating that when one doesn't understand what another is saying, one should indicate such, and utilize another method of communication.

Later in his office I formulated a way of presenting an example of what I meant. He said a number of things in an effort to explain why certain items were displayed on a form; at the same time I chose to fumble in my wallet, extracting heaps of crumped papers, while appearing distracted by the volume, and also garbled something, and then asked; "Did I understand what you were saying?"

His response was silence, and I knew why he wasn't saying a word. While still appearing enveloped with the extent of the paperwork I'd discovered in my wallet, I repeated the question; "Did I understand what you were saying?"

I noticed he had a pen positioned above a series of numbers, and I knew that instead of using words to clarify the issue at hand, he would merely direct my eyes to the nature of the problem.

I then had the audacity to say; "What you are doing follows common sense; if one method of communication isn't working, formulate another."

He then responded by saying; "Are you accusing me of something?"

At that point I decided to abruptly change my mode of behaviour, because the bank manager had now distinguished something I mentioned under my breath while approaching his office; "You hired these people; you're responsible."

I knew he'd assimilated my message, and I felt I'd made my point; I then decided to turn the table around, and say;

"No, quite the opposite; I was praising you for acknowledging the nature of the problem."

He actually apologized for misinterpreting my words. I hadn't accused him of anything; I had proven my point. The receptionist, whom he had deemed fit, (qualified), for her position, had **lied;** and he had sought to cover up this lie, and felt so threatened by my recognizing the underlying root cause, he was willing to close all my accounts to insure another incident of a similar nature would not transpire.

Truth be told, had she, the receptionist, been more interested in providing a service proficiently, instead of protecting her image, her "self", my issue would have been resolved with greater alacrity.

Ask yourself, since I have declared the above; how many have walked away from this receptionist's desk believing they have the answer they've seeking, but were actually told a load of rubbish, but due to her managing to sound so impressive, they believed it was true? I happen to know quite a bit about banking, primarily due to complications that had arisen in the past, and became aware, practically immediately, that the receptionist had no idea what she was talking about.

Consider now the question; is it logical to assume someone will walk away from a desk, with no clear destination in mind, merely due to another's tone of voice? Obviously not!

The manager was defending a lie, complicit in it; and due to a desire to continue telling this lie, he was prepared to use any means at his disposal to get rid of the person able to expose the truth. Why was he so insecure? – Because I was in the right, which he would later acknowledge by declaring that he felt persecuted in my presence; thus, the words; "are you accusing me of something?" I think he knew the answer; YES – you totally lack common sense.

How could he have handled this problem better? He didn't know how. He may have been unaware of the extent to which he'd accepted his own ignorance, (I'd encountered a very similar situation with two of his other employees). He was not facing facts, but lying about the degree to which those involved were qualified.

It was too much, in other words, for his Ego to handle; which was as precious to him, as it was to the young woman behind the desk, and each was prepared to use whatever tools at their disposal in an effort to not recognize, be cognizant of, their own inadequacies. At any cost each was prepared to persecute the one exposing the lie in order to protect the image they had developed of themselves, and hoped others would recognize as the truth.

Once considering all the factors mentioned above, it is easy to calculate what the issue was; which happens to be the first step in eliminating the matter; the second is discovering a remedy. What I mean by this is that when you take something away, it has to be replaced with something else; much the same as a flat tire on a car.

The problem was not my tone of voice, nor was it the possibility the receptionist wasn't aware of the meaning of the word "invalid"; the issue is one of "LIES", and an unwillingness to appreciate the detrimental impact such behaviour has upon others. The term "demean", therefore, is fitting under the circumstance. Telling lies, obviously, shouldn't be praised – this is common sense, as I pointed out to the manager; but I was told that demeaning the staff at his bank cannot be tolerated, and that is the reason why they are neither admonished, nor reprimanded, in any manner, despite the cost another must bear as a consequence.

This is the very essence of madness, and the manager became cognizant of this when he used the words; "are you accusing me of something?" He knew precisely the point I had directed his attention toward, and he was making an attempt to diffuse my "offensive" observations, all the while knowing full well, of course, that due to his previous threat, I wouldn't pursue the matter further.

What I have clearly shown is that guarding their "Ego" was such a precious undertaking for both, nothing was considered too extreme as a means to defend it – such is the root cause of narcissism, and because of this, both are disconnected from their fellow man. They are entirely enveloped in their own circumstance, which also explains the degree to which each is ignorant.

They have no interest beyond the dimensions of the small bubble that represents their world, which is their lives; to expect any form of genuine nourishment/love from either is entirely unrealistic, and if one does believe such is possible, the idea is based on delusional thought. The notion of either being capable of any form of logical thought is ridiculous, as well.

The entire "system" enveloping our world today is designed to make sure a connection between people is not possible, although the illusion formulated is that people are learning to empathize more and more, and at an ever increasing rate.

The development of this conception is primarily due to the work of "marketers", who have assiduously instilled this delusion into the common man's mind. People presently develop attachments to electrical objects, believing they are akin to humans made of flesh, bone, and blood, whether it be a cell phone, a blackberry, computer, T.V. screen, and other such objects that people while away their time using or simply staring at.

The most unfortunate aspect of our present circumstance is that practically everybody has developed the belief that they are communicating ideas; but this, indubitably, is not the case. English, for example, unbeknownst to both parents, and their offspring, is no longer being taught in schools. The most explicit evidence of such being the case is the fact that when you enter the grounds of practically any university campus, you'll notice signs posted throughout regarding assistance being offered to teach grammar, how to formulate a paragraph, and write an essay.

The truth is that people have been brainwashed to believe the gobble de goop nonsense that spews out of their mouths actually makes sense. I am reminded presently of the "Tower of Babel" in The Bible;

abbreviations of words, deleting words that are essential in formulating a sentence, ensure there can be no exchange of worthwhile ideas.

I have provided the fundamental reason as to why, as most in the world would openly admit, nothing works well these days, or as it should; people don't care about how their actions affect others.

The word, "care", can be defined as attending to something, taking an interest. People who have become narcissists continually pamper themselves; they are only interested in their own lives; such being the case, and the system presently operating in the world being designed to enable the manufacture of such a mentality; how would it then be possible for any product to be manufactured as it should, or service provided proficiently?

Is it in any way surprising that the quality, and the standard, of both products and services are continually declining, and at an ever increasing rate, (the question is rhetorical).

Picture all the elements noted as being fused to create a solid metal ball that is released from the top of the Tower of Pisa. The rate at which it descends will increase due to gravity. When it hits the ground, it would have reached its maximum speed of acceleration. Things cannot get any worse, the world, (the metal ball), has already slammed into the ground. Humanity, therefore, has encountered the same, but because mankind is so enveloped in itself, there was no recognition that this had occurred.

The evidence of such being the case is, without exception, everywhere you go. If anyone were to attempt to point out that something isn't quite right, and needs to be improved upon, the response most likely will be harsh, and this is due to the recognition that the effort required for such to transpire is so great, it is not perceived as viable.

Picture what I've described as a train, and someone tells the driver a sharp turn is up ahead; even if he has brakes, the driver will require a certain distance in which to apply those brakes in order to reach a safe speed to make the turning without the train toppling over. People, most sadly, do not even have brakes, (figuratively speaking), and this is why they really have no awareness that their lives are wrecks, and they can only wreck the lives of others they come in contact with.

When someone tells you someone else is only at a certain location in order to get a pay-cheque, what they are in fact telling you is that the person is a narcissist, and, therefore, **evil**; he/she is not a loving, loyal, or self-sacrificial, creature. The person in question does the barest minimum required to obtain a pay-cheque, and if the ability to acquire that pay-cheque is perceived to be compromised in any way, measures will be taken immediately, if possible, to eradicate the conceived threat, and that is the reason why the incident I described in the bank arose; both the manager, and the receptionist, are **evil**. If you believe anything to the contrary, that is due to the overwhelming influence advertisements have had upon you; in other words, you bought the lie, and much the same as the free-falling ball, or the train thundering along the track, you cannot stop believing the utter complete nonsense, although you have been provided evidence that the claims made couldn't possibly be true!!

To make a comparison; a person notices someone kicking their foot against a brick wall, and informs the person about the damage he's doing to his foot, (the blood visibly dipping from the sole of his shoe, is more than sufficient evidence), but because he has no awareness of the damage he is inflicting upon himself, primarily due to the foot having gone completely numb, you can't stop him kicking the wall, because he doesn't even know how; and why should he, (thinking to himself), if no damage is being done? What's the sense?

I have also detailed how the expression, "biting off the hand that feeds you", came about. It is due to the person who's receiving help not taking into consideration the circumstance of the person offering help; in essence, what takes over is **greed**. The person offering assistance, therefore, withdraws the hand that's presenting the offering, not just to protect himself, but to have the opportunity to help others in some capacity in the future.

Narcissism, ultimately, is self-destructive; if you don't scratch another person's back, no one will scratch your back; therefore, people create their own insecurities, and as a consequence wonder what will happen when they require help, and there is no one around to offer it? And, frankly, they already know the answer to this quandary; nobody is going to extend any form of assistance.

In order to picture how this feels; imagine travelling in a car on a snowy, cold, winter night, through a desolate region of countryside, when you have an engine breakdown; what are you going to do?

At this point, I can inform members of my audience why people carry cell phones wherever they go, and are continually "text messaging"; it is due to the insecurity derived from disconnecting oneself from others, and also explains why people hoard; thus, the expression, "saving things for a rainy day". Each acts as a "security blanket" protecting the person from an indefinable threat lying somewhere within the indeterminable future.

I provided a picture of someone harming himself by repeatedly slamming his foot into a wall, and the foot subsequently becoming numb due to the repeated abuse. The body habituates itself to pain in order to survive. It will provide a warning, but only up to a point, then a line is crossed that turns off the caution signal; thus, people are entirely unacquainted with the level of damage they are inflicting upon themselves; and that is why there is such a thing as phantom pain, or the sense that a limb is still present after it has been severed.

I would also like to remind my audience that the Monolith deliberately sought to transform people into objects that can be easily manipulated, so they act in accordance with their will; hence, the dimming of minds, and the weakening of bodies.

I'd like to stipulate that the vast majority of those who believe they are extraordinarily physically fit, are quite the opposite, and this is due to an excessive number of workouts, and workouts that are too strenuous, or a combination of both; but due to "nutritional supplements", "vitamin pills", and certain drugs, and so on and so forth, people have bought the illusion they are physically fit. They believe they are fine physical specimens merely due to an image of themselves they consider appealing that is seen in a mirror.

All athletes, (not those who engage in today's sports world), who have long careers, are careful to note how their body is responding to exercises, and the duration of those exercises. Even the best can sometimes overstep the mark, and have had to retire early because of this; case in point, Bjorn Borg, ("Ice man", "Ice Borg"), who admitted he had, to use his terminology, "burned himself out", and this was due to adhering to a regimen that was excessive. He was known to "practice", (a term used to note everything connected to the profession of tennis), 12 hours a day.

One of my tennis heroes is Guillermo Vilas, ("The young bull of the Pampas"), who also happened to be a poet. He declared that he believed he didn't have an abundance of "natural talent", but rather his success was due to working hard. He never, as far as I am aware, "practiced" more than 5 hours a day. It is quite likely he managed to keep a healthy balance in his day to day affairs due to having numerous interests comparably important to him as tennis.

If one were to comprehensively survey the lifestyle of those who are "celebrity athletes", one will no doubt discover an imbalance in their lives; their minds arc too focused on their profession, and whether they wish to admit it to themselves, or not, this is primarily induced by their love of "celebrity", "being a star", and the riches that go along with it. This also helps to explain why so many celebrities in their chosen field, (sports, actors, musicians), are so pitiful at what they claim to be so good at.

A great many actresses in Hollywood, for example, have resorted to plastic surgery and such things as Botox, to sell perfumes, clothing, make-up, credit cards, among other products, in order to stay in the "spot light", which, quite obviously, diminishes their ability to act at the same time.

It is quite incredible, as far as I am concerned, that the general public is almost entirely unaware of how miserable, as a result, they are at doing their job as an actor; (or maybe they are a mirror of themselves, and it seems quite natural to them?). Most, I would hope, will wonder how they managed not to notice what I have detailed.

The disconnection people make between themselves and others, due to greed, gluttony, and selfishness, can only incapacitate due to the damage they continually inflict on their minds and bodies. Unfortunately, people are not even close to realizing all the methods, tactics, and devices, used to damage their capacity to behave promptly, proficiently, and accurately. Marketers, of course, in their bid to acquire the largest amount of wealth, (investing the smallest amount possible, while reaping the most enormous rewards imaginable), will focus their attention on the weaker subject, (Electra Complex); and that would be women; the following will illustrate the extent to which they have taken hold of today's female population.

Jon & Vangelis
The friends of Mr. Cairo

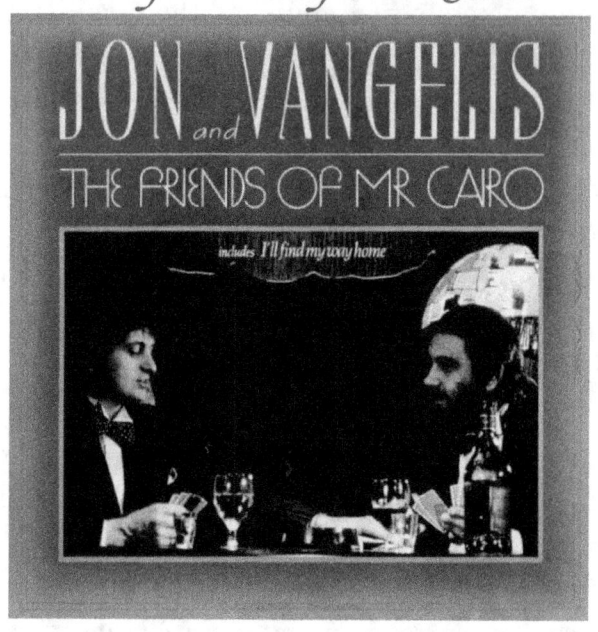

Citizen Kane came fast and quickly
Conquerin ol' New York City
Pokin fun at superstition
Media became television

Give me Cagney anyday
Or Jimmy Steward for President

Or Edward 'G' and all those guys
Who always shoot between the eyes
Between the eyes
Between the eyes

The Trinity Manifesto; Vol. I

I frequent a university campus practically every day, and recently I thought of, what I consider to be, a fitting title for this establishment; "The Parade of Black Tights". Practically all the women on campus are accustomed to wearing the same type of attire from one day to the next; a wardrobe consisting almost exclusively of dull, muted, tones; dim coloured tops, and, (except on the days they wear jeans), black, skin tight, pants, (I think of this as their "corporate uniforms") - due to the degree the pants are sheer, it is most obvious that almost all of the women are accustomed to wearing either a thong, or no underwear at all, on a regular basis. They also, without exception, have a habit of placing their dirty shoes, or feet, (with or without socks), on the seats they are sitting on, as well as sitting on the floor; walking barefoot into bathrooms is not an uncommon sight either.

The obvious consequence of these habits is that they are "infecting" themselves; their most vulnerable part; the channel through which a new life form greets the world. By not wearing panties, or wearing those of light colour, the "infected" mucous will seep into the black fabric, but they will not see it, and it will also likely reach the seat others will sit on later.

Who can stop them? What I have discovered is that if I protest in any way feet being placed upon a seat, I will greet an unsympathetic response; no other male will back me up; and I am likely to be kicked off the premises by security.

A lot of the males on the campus think it's great that so many of the female student body are promiscuous, (being a "slut" is customary now, and is not, in the vast majority of cases, considered to be cause for the slightest bit of shame).

Now that I have declared all that I have, it is easy to formulate an answer as to why approximately 50% of marriages end in divorce, and why children are neglected, abandoned, and abused, in the numbers they most evidently are; the parents, man and wife, are not attending to, taking an interest in, anything other than themselves.

Let me provide an example of how most are not aware, and do not comprehend, the nature of what is around them, and because of this relationships are bound to fail, and their offspring will never have anything of worth to offer society.

A man approaches the receptionist at the bank that I noted previously, and thinks, "This woman is a catch". She looks great, her smile is welcoming, her perfume so alluring, and when she bends over, he can see practically an entire exposed breast. He's in heaven – or so he thinks!

She looks up his bank information, and her eyes immediately light up. The fellow in front of her is a good catch; there's an enormous amount of cash in several accounts.

"What can I do for you today?" She asks with a twinkle in her eye. More than ever he can appreciate how great he must appear through her eyes.

There will never be a genuine relationship between these two people. They are both narcissists; but who of the two will pay a greater price for engaging with the other? My answer, without a shadow of doubt, is the man.

Healthy, productive, children will never be the outcome of this relationship. If she doesn't get enough of what she wants, money, or sex, for example, she will seek it elsewhere. If a man should come along who appears to have more to offer than she's getting already, she will bond to that object in a heartbeat, and most likely, due to knowing how **wrong** her conduct is, will attempt to hide it for a period of time, and, thus, it can be named, for want of another term, an "affair".

If the man then wants a divorce – **look out**; because there is no justice in the legal system these days. If she can take every cent they've accumulated as a couple, she will. This object, that is such a pleasure to look at, and speaks in such a soft voice, is thoroughly disconnected from her fellow man, and is, I repeat, **evil.**

If more evidence is required to prove my point, here it is; look at all the sites on the internet, for instance, concerning women offering sex; to give an example, "discreet 'housewives" looking for sex". They present pictures of the goods they have to offer. Go into practically any grocery store, and look at the number of magazine racks filled with pornographic magazines. Women love the attention, and can also get paid for taking their clothes off as well; but why, women love to ask, do men have such dirty minds, and look at such filth? The answer is because women keep putting their bare derrieres in men's faces.

The advertising hides the truth, which is ugly, and despicable; advertising campaigns of this nature are as comprehensive, and widespread, as one could possibly imagine.

Men often complain about women confusing sex with love; I don't think there is confusion – it is a matter of the value you place on what you have to offer. If sex is all you've got to extend, then you will see it as the defining element in a relationship, and, therefore, when "cheating" occurs, thereby creating a split between people; it is not because he/she got "it" from someone else, which causes the disruption, but the deception used to acquire it, which results in a loss of trust.

Men, quite obviously, are demonstrating that a genuine relationship, what should be called "love", involves elements that are just as, if not more, important than sex.

For all the reasons I have detailed above, one of the Commandments is not to covet another man's wife.

Men and women are different, and for people to stay together, and ultimately learn to nourish themselves, and also be able to rear children properly, these differences need to be respected.

Christ is purported to have said that looking at a woman other than your wife with lust is a sin, (actually, he is reported to have stated that looking at any woman with lust is a sin).

Focusing so much attention on appearances is, by its very nature, superficial, and reveals at the same time the depth to which a person's mind is capable of appreciating the complexity of matters.

Matthew 5:27-28 (KJV)

"You have heard that it was said, 'You shall not commit adultery.' But I tell you that anyone who looks at a woman lustfully has already committed adultery with her in his heart."

This is in full agreement with a Commandment included in the Ten given to Moses. It is one of the Laws of the cosmos; it is The Divine Order.

The word "command" can mean that if you break it, do not observe it, you will pay a price; and I have fully explained why this is the case.

The Tenth Commandment, (Exodus 20:17, KJV):

Thou shalt not covet thy neighbour's house, thou shalt not covet thy neighbour's wife, nor his manservant, nor his maidservant, nor his ox, nor his ass, nor any thing that is thy neighbours.

Discovery

iscover your being, find your
heart;
    know your fellow man,
though he seems lost in the dark.

A passage is hidden; where does it lead?
It doesn't matter!
Wait till the light passes through,
then you'll find it all leads to you.

Extrapolate, manipulate, cogitate,
    divide;
I'll find the solution when I have
    nothing left to hide.

The Mr. Roger's version of;
"It's a beautiful day in the neighbourhood,
it's a beautiful day today", in an office building.

"THE CIVIL SERVANT"

THE CHARACTERS

Ben: (Department Manager)
Cindy: (office clerk)
SCENE ONE: (Every day is a re-creation of Scene One)

Play takes place on a nondescript office floor consisting of rows of cubicles, each containing a rectangular metal desk. Ben approaches Cindy's cubicle. The time is approximately 9:30 am. Cindy has been quietly seated at her cubicle since 9:00 am filing her nails.

Ben: Morning, Cindy. I have a job for you to do.

Cindy reluctantly places her file on her desk before responding.

Cindy: Great! I've been waiting for something to do!
The sarcasm in her remark is obvious.

Ben slaps a manila folder, half an inch thick, in front of Cindy. It is held together with a thick, red, rubber band.

Ben: This file is closed; we, in management, like to call it "inactive".
He speaks with a drawl, as if he's from one of the States in the south of the U.S. – on the other hand, it is far more likely he's had a few drinks this morning; which also helps to explain his difficulty walking in a straight line.

Cindy immediately attempts to get the rubber band off the folder.

Cindy: Great! I was gettin kinda bored.

Ben: No, don't open the file; as I told you, it's closed.

Cindy: You've assigned me to a folder I can't open?

Ben: That's correct; and if you like, you have the entire day to work on it.

Cindy: I'm new here; I don't understand. How can I work on it, if I'm not allowed to open it?

Ben: Cindy, I should tell you that unlike so many other offices, we actually encourage creative thought, and new ideas. I'm sure you'll discover for yourself what management expects from you in no time at all.

Cindy: You've assigned me to a file that's "inactive", and for an entire day?

Ben: Yes. We're understaffed right now, and I'm afraid you'll have to tackle this assignment all by yourself.

Cindy: It's nice to know I'm needed; but since I can't open this file, could I get another file for my nails? The one I brought with me is gettin kindna dull.

Ben: We always like to accommodate the special needs of our employees. I'll have someone bring you a fresh file in a few minutes. It's important to management that you feel comfortable; with our limited number of employees, we try to do whatever we can, within reason, of course, to insure each can be as productive as possible.

Cindy: How can I work on a file I can't even open, that you've told me, is closed?

Ben: Cindy, you're agitating yourself by asking so many questions that are redundant. Rest assured management knows what it's doing. The policies we have in place are designed to make sure that no matter the number of staff we have on duty, the most work possible is being accomplished.

Cindy: The file is "inactive", as you put it; I would assume by not being allowed to open it, at the end of the work day, it will remain "inactive".

Ben: As I said, Cindy; management has everything well in hand; no changes are necessary – we're trained experts.

Cindy: Will I getting a different closed file tomorrow?

Ben: I can tell you're new here, Cindy; you're asking a lot of questions. You can only work on another file, when you've finished with this file.

Cindy: How long, typically, would I have to **not** work on a file, before I move onto another?

Ben: Management decides that. Don't concern yourself with such minor details...You look lovely today, by the way; black suits you, you'll fit in well here; but, I can see strain on your face, and that doesn't reflect well on management. What I suggest is you simply have faith. Do you go to church?

Cindy: Oh, yes! I'm a Mormon. I love Jesus!

Ben: Wonderful! Then you already know what I mean when I say, "have faith". We're trying to make a "positive" change here. We respect everybody's opinion equally...Someone will bring a new file for your nails, and at the end of the day, maybe an hour earlier, I'll pick up the folder containing the file. Oh, and please, keep the file clean; cleanliness is next to godliness, don't you know!

Cindy: If you say so.

Ben: That's what I want to hear. Have a little more faith in your fellow man. We're all a part of the same community, and we have to get along.

Cindy: I agree.

Ben turns around, and starts to walk away, while raising a hand as a farewell gesture.

Ben: Have a good day, Cindy.

Cindy: I sure will Ben. You have a good day, as well. It's nice to be a part of a team.

A pause occurs while a thought rises in Cindy's mind; then, she speaks in a louder voice, to make sure Ben can hear as he continues to walk away.

Cindy: If I receive a text message, is it O.K. if I answer it?

Ben: As long as you get your work done by the end of the day, I'll say today, that will be around 3 pm, I see no reason why not. We understand that you have a life outside of the office, and other responsibilities. Deal with them as quickly as possible, and that way you won't be distracted. We expect the highest quality of work from you.

Cindy: Have a good day.

Ben doesn't respond; he's too far away to hear her farewell greeting.

THE END

The Trinity Manifesto; Vol. I

The message behind the Play, "The Civil Servant", is that if two ideas contradict one another, the message is nullified.

It's good to keep busy, though; after all, idle hands do the work of the Devil.

A man's capacity to survive is largely dependent on the degree to which his mind is able to operate proficiently; the longer he is able to live, greater in his ability to enrich his life.

The world, in a manner of speaking, has been dying, falling into an ever deeper state of decay, since the conclusion of the Second World War. Man, once given the capacity to be the noblest of creatures, is now a cretin in the vast preponderance of cases; unable to successfully accomplish, relatively speaking, even the simplest of tasks.

When a man continually behaves in a moral, truthful, manner, his thoughts, actions, and deeds, are in sympathy; they are synchronized. The collected body of energy, to make a comparison, is flowing cohesively in the same direction; if one were to make the analogy of it being a body of water, it has the capacity to displace objects; picture a feather travelling of the surface of a swiftly flowing current within a stream.

When a man lies, deceives, steals, or in any way consistently behaves in an immoral manner, the current of energy is at cross purposes; picture streams flowing from different directions clashing as they bombard one another. The capacity to move an object in a definite direction, along a certain course, is no longer a possibility; a feather will most likely be sucked below the surface, and trapped within the currents of water churning below.

The person that decides to behave in an immoral manner will inevitably damage his capacity to reason, acquire dementia, to use a medical term, due to nerves, "wires", in the brain crossing one another, and short circuiting; unless new synaptic connections are made, and due to a weakening recognition of the cause behind the trouble there will be a diminished interest in doing so, the condition is permanent, and will progressively grow worse..

The Buddha, Siddhartha Gautama, spoke of Four Noble Truths, and an Eightfold Noble Path, which includes "right livelihood"; he is referring to that which encourages moral behaviour.

Personally I would never be a member of any organization that would have me as a member – and that's no joke!

For My Opinion

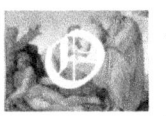

*pinions
reveal a perspective
you would like others to
see.*

*An idea once hidden is now revealed;
It has now become the real deal.*

*One by one, a section is taken away.
The core of what you believe
is there after that last peel.*

*The world is captured in my eye.
How unique this all is to me.
Come here within;
join me as I examine the plenteous wonders
the world has given.*

*Light and dark, shades of grey;
colours that appear only in May.
Gathered together they are joy, care, and
love;
the only things required to be gay.*

*I see you, you see me;
entwined as one we will forever be.
Regardless of the ignorance between;
forever buying things
will cost us far more than the seen fee.*

The Trinity Manifesto; Vol. I

*People gather, separate, congregate in
squares,
quarters, corners, wherever;
the hidden is expressed in each and every
opinion.
In none is truth.
Only when we all become one,
will all be seen the same forever.*

Unwise Behaviour

istreatment is so unkind,
and, obviously, and
evidently, very unwise;
yet so many follow this horrendous course.

It goes against nature.
  Look at your surroundings;
the evidence is there all around,
with haste,
mankind has robbed the goods of the
Earth.

The Fall is near,
  this day will soon come.
The possibility to create, give, love, will be
entirely gone.
Is there, could there, be anything else,
that could make us feel glum?

Disparaging, negative, destructive,
menacing words,
are used with reckless, thoughtless,
disregard.
Many call these simply acts of negligence;
but they still hurt.

Truth be told, its nature is far from
complex.
Many wise men in the past gave warnings;
they told us of the things we should avoid;
but, again and again, we've ignored.

The Trinity Manifesto; Vol. I

*These things cause me to wonder and
perplex;
it would have been so simple to listen then
follow,
but ignorance allowed this not to be so.
So, as dreadful as it may sound,
once these people die,
to hell itself they will go.*

Peter Gabriel / Big Tiime

I'm on my way I'm making it, Huh!
I've got to let it show, Hey!
So much larger than life

I'm gonna watch it growing
Hey hey hey heyyyyyyy

The place where I come from is a small town
They think so small, they use small words
But not me, I'm smarter than that,
I worked it out
I'll be stretching my mouth to let those big words come right out.
I've had enough, I'm getting out
To the city, the big big city
I'll be a big noise with all the big boys, so much stuff I will own
And I will pray to a big god, as I kneel in the big church.

Misunderstandings

isunderstandings,
are the nature of disputes.
One thinks he's right,
the other believes the opposite.
He is more than wrong.
There have been far too many occasions
when,
as a result, a man has been hung.

The difference is knowledge.
We have the right to disagree,
but the important thing is to take account,
but never dare charge a fee.

The love of the self brings death to one's
soul;
as a result also he beside you,
as well as He above;
meaning, the Being that is peace,
that we often express with the flight of a
dove.

A Circle to Witness Then Dismiss

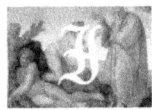 n a circle they sit claiming
that life is a pit,
and quite often they feel
they want to quit!

They claim they are here to listen to what
others have to say,
but often, if questioned,
will state, "They didn't say that, did
they?"

Whether one chooses to refute or rebuke,
they will continue to live as they've
always done;
their minds closed to the wisdom that
surrounds.
Point them in any direction,
and they will claim you are a hound.

What is the point in speaking a truth
when all around people are left deaf,
as though they are living in a closed booth?

This is the price we pay,
for allowing people to live in complete
utter dismay.
Don't extend a hand to others who see this
in no way grand.
This extension of aid they will not take,

The Trinity Manifesto; Vol. I

but rob you they will of the money in your
    pocket,
or a cake you have yet to bake.

For them a meaningful nugget of
    knowledge
means nothing more than a bowl of soup,
or a clump of thick porridge.

The Trinity Manifesto; Vol. I

Dark cannot detect light, but light can detect dark.

John 1:5
*And the light shineth in darkness, and the darkness
comprehended it not.
King James Bible, "Authorized Version",
Cambridge Edition*

The Trinity Manifesto; Vol. I

George Harrison/My Sweet Lord

I really want to see you
Really want to be with you
Really want to see you Lord
But it takes so long, my Lord

My sweet lord
Hm, my lord
Hm, my lord

I really want to know you
Really want to go with you
Really want to show you lord
That it won't take long, my lord (hallelujah)

John Lennon/Paul McCartney

Second Side Abbey Road

Oh, yeah! Alright!
Are you gonna be in my dreams tonight?

And, in the end
The love you take
Is equal to the love you make.

John Lennon/Imagine

Imagine there's no heaven
It's easy if you try
No hell below us
Above us only sky
Imagine all the people living for today

Imagine there's no countries
It isn't hard to do
Nothing to kill or die for
And no religion too
Imagine all the people living life in peace

Lessons of Life

 have stood in a harbour, on
a deck
of a mighty ship.
Seagulls were there,
as well as the smell of the dead
carried on the surface of the sea.

Beauty is countered by ugliness,
motion by that which is still.
One by one we learn the lessons life has to
offer that fulfill.

Feeling secure will happen
when gathered together is the wisdom
contained in each;
then, no matter where you may be,
only light will be contained in that which
you see.

Why is it so often said, a dog is a man's best friend?
I had a dog once, his name was McDougal.
He's gone now; where, I don't know,
But in my heart he remains
Here with me forever.
Amen.
I assume ghosts are real, so now I think of him as Casper.

A Dog Named Casper

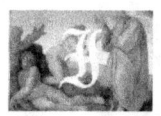 **once had a dog
that has now passed away.**

In fields he did roam.
Casper was his name.

Carefree, fearlessly, he did play.
To this day I remember him so well.
In my mind he appears as somewhat a ghost.
Casper was his name.

Though anxious I could sometimes be,
he made the mist clear so I could see.

There can be a shadow that appears as
light.
It dispenses the fear
that can often fill me with fright.

Among leaves fallen from trees he did
scurry, and wander.

The Trinity Manifesto; Vol. I

Through streams, and pastures green, he
    would saunter.
I can't imagine a creature of whom I could
    grow fonder.

His fur fluttered in gusts of Autumn
    wind,
along with the twittering birds,
they created a song nature could sing.

At night when life has left me with
    worries, and strain,
it is Casper that visits from some far off
    realm.
In a dream he shows me the way to lessen
    my pain.

In so many ways he and I were alike.
His bark was never close to a bite.

I glance at his picture in a frame;
what a glorious, magical, sight!
It gives me hope that some day
all will have a chance to be made right.

He appeared in my life when all seemed
    dark, and grey;
like an angel fallen from heaven above:
what more can I say.

I watched as he grew, aged, and became
    old.
A lifetime passed before my eyes;
teaching me so much;
most of all what it means to be strong and
    bold.

The Trinity Manifesto; Vol. I

When his days reached their last,
I thought all was lost;
where did my friend go I grown to know?
Now I have to learn to be my own boss;
Casper is no longer here to snuggle softly
    by my side.

In a way I sense he never left me;
within crevices, around corners, behind
    doors, he hides;
much like a guardian who guides.

As I rush through thick, tall, grass,
trying to reach a place I can call home,
I realize more each day I've already
    arrived;
safely cradled in love that is my humble
    abode.

Pictured in my imagination is a dog that
    stood stoic and strong.
I can feel his presence,
though, at times, I weep, because for him I
    so long.

I have learned to face the world with
    continuing fascination.
Eagerly I wait for each day to begin;
no longer bothering with
manufactured schemes that fuel
    procrastination.

A friend he once was, and will always
    remain.
Much like him,

The Trinity Manifesto; Vol. I

I will always continue to be the same.
Deep within I have light that shines as if
made of gold.

The dog that sat by my side, is here to stay; Casper was his name.

 ghost is a spirit you quite often see at night.

It might be your friend, but still you feel fright.

Why should this be?
Many stories have been told that, quite simply, aren't true.
They appear when times are hard, and all seems made of blue.
Then again, it could be when everything seems fresh, and quite new.

Things hover, doors shut;
watch carefully, and with a little luck,
you'll discover your long lost hockey puck.
What a charm it is to perceive these

The Trinity Manifesto; Vol. I

precious wonders.
So many men have for reams of time on
these things pondered.

How could it be, happen, that objects
move without a seen cause?
To me, the answer is obvious; a will
from a mind creates this force.

Symbols, signs,
are left for those who wish to discern
their meaning.
At nightfall there await mysteries,
that beseech to reach the curious
soul.

The Most High Is Within

 ruths
are seen in proof.

Is God in us?
Does He guide us
so we follow the right path?
We know so little, it may be just as well be
a route followed by a local bus.

Strange things lie all around.
We haven't a chance of understanding
every minute part.
Just place your hand on your heart,
swear you'll always try to do what's right
and proper,
then, largely unbeknownst to you,
you will experience, perceive, and create,
wonders that belong to so few.

Look around!
He is here, there, and everywhere.
Most of all experience Him within.
There lies all that can be given!

Colin Wilson

Life itself is an exile. The way home is not the way back.

The average man is a conformist, accepting miseries and disasters with the stoicism of a cow standing in the rain.

Religion, mysticism and magic all spring from the same basic 'feeling' about the universe; a sudden feeling of meaning, which human beings sometimes 'pick up' accidently, as your radio might pick up some unknown station. Poets feel that we are cut off from meaning by a thick, lead ball, and that sometimes for no reason we can understand the wall seems to vanish and we are suddenly overwhelmed with the sense of the infinite interestingness of things.

Stephen King

Monsters are real, and ghosts are real too. They live inside us, and sometimes, they win.

Dean Koontz

I believe I was a dog in a past life. That the only thing that would explain why I snack on Purina Dog Chow.

Ann Rice

Even if a ghost is ripping a house to pieces, throwing tin pans all over, pouring water on pillows, making clocks chime at all hours, mortals will accept any "natural explanation" offered, no matter how absurd, rather than the obvious supernatural one, for what is going on.

Peter Straub

The world is full of ghosts, and some are still people.

Arthur Conan Doyle

Watson: Then you are yourself inclining to the supernatural explanation.
Holmes: if Dr. Mortimer's surmise should be correct, and we are dealing with forces outside the ordinary laws of Nature, there is an end to our investigation. But we are bound to exhaust all other hypotheses before falling back upon this one.

When any man seeks to better the lives of others, not just those in his own time, but the generations to follow, an energy transcends his body that has decayed and passed away, and fills us with hope that one day we will all be free, and live life as it was meant to be.

A MAN FOR ALL TIMES

One man devoted his life to better the lives of others.
The ripples of hope he brought to people everywhere can remain alive
and well, if we make his dream our own, and wish to one day live in a
world where no man suffers oppression, goes without food, or clothing to
keep warm.
Our world will only survive if we all aim to achieve this goal, otherwise
we will inevitably fail to sustain the human species.
We need the courage and strength to abolish the injustices that take
place every day, all over the globe.

Jewish proverb;
"Ask not for a lighter burden,
but broader shoulders.

Winston

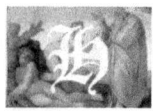 e encouraged men to fight,
on the seas, and oceans, on
hills, plains,
among the clouds suspended in the sky.

All he needed were words,
and the power to present;
not once did he use potions!
He always said what he meant.

His character was murky to most.
He had a softer side,
but also often found reason to boast.

Many thought him harsh, lacking
compassion;
all told, these thoughts
should have long gone out of fashion.

Wisdom he held,
the future he could often predict;
how did he manage to do all this?
Favouring liquors, chomping on cigars,
was how he managed to keep fit.

He stood apart in so many ways.
Loving the company of others,
dinners he held in his ideal Cottage.
Others felt welcome, never as if a hostage.

The Trinity Manifesto; Vol. I

Being in his presence was the rich reward.
Denying themselves this gift, they could
    not afford.

Often, it would seem,
Churchill found the remarks of others
    amusing,
and their opinions of little interest;
but his personality they thoroughly adored,
and his charms were all so soothing.

How could he possibly be perceived as a
    pest?
History reveals he made men become their
    best!

Nothing is this world is free;
everything of value has to be earned.
Man, as The Lord instructed, must toil till the end of his days.
The greatest among men serve as examples to emulate and imitate; they
remind us that The Lord resides in each of us,
and if we simply strive to always do what is just,
He will grant us His sweet heavenly grace,
And bless us until we find our final resting place.

Missa Solemnis

Day 6

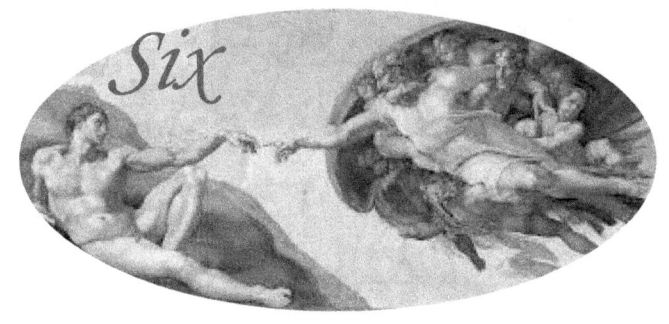

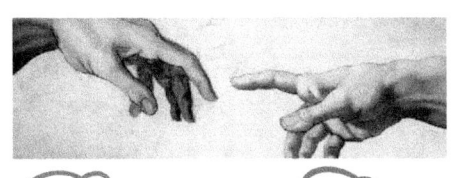

Peace will Come

When man learns how to
Live with his fellow man.
In order for that to occur,
He must first learn about his own nature.
It is not matter, but Spirit.
Once man realizes this,
He can be at peace with himself,
And he can also live in harmony with his fellow man.
Our Spirit is the same as The Lord's,
He is everywhere,
And He is within each of us.
His Laws are our Laws;
There are 10,
And they must be adhered to
At all times.

EXODUS
THE TEN COMMANDMENTS

And God spake all these words, saying,
I am the Lord thy God, which have brought thee out of
the land of Egypt, out of the house of bondage.

1. Thou shalt have no other gods before me.
2. Thou shalt not make unto thee any graven image, or
any likeness of anything that is in heaven above, or that
is the earth beneath, or that is in the water under the
earth:
Thou shalt not bow down thyself to them, nor serve
them: for I the Lord thy God am a jealous God, visiting
the iniquity of the fathers upon the children unto the
third and fourth generation of them that hate me;
And showing mercy unto thousands of them that love
me, and keep my commandments.
3. Thou shalt not take the name of the Lord thy God in
vain: for the Lord will not hold him guiltless that taketh
his name in vain.
4. Remember the Sabbath day, to keep it holy. Six days
shalt thou labor, and do all thy work:
but the seventh day is the Sabbath of the Lord thy God:
in it thou shalt not do any work, thou, nor thy son, nor
thy daughter, thy manservant, nor thy maidservant, nor
thy cattle, nor thy stranger that is within thy gates:
for in six days the Lord made heaven and earth, the sea,
and all that in them is, and rested the seventh day:
wherefore the Lord blessed the Sabbath day, and
hallowed it.

5. Honor thy father and thy mother: that thy days may be long upon the land which the Lord thy God giveth thee.

6. Thou shalt not kill.

7. Thou shalt not commit adultery.

8. Thou shalt not steal.

9. Thou shalt not bear false witness against thy neighbor.

10. Thou shalt not covet thy neighbor's house, thou shalt not covet thy neighbor's wife, nor his manservant, nor his maidservant, nor his ox, nor his ass, nor any thing that is thy neighbour's.

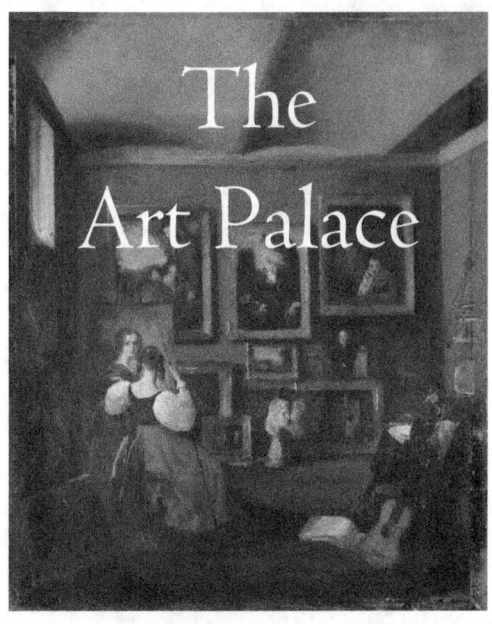

The Art Palace

'

Crediton is a small town, also a beautiful one, with many sights that can easily delight the eye. Inside there stands a cathedral built centuries ago, and within are the memories, reflections, prayers, and gifts, of those who mourn, grieve, offer praise, and seek to understand better the "One" who leads us all.

There are other places of a similar nature to be found in this town, but they are smaller in stature, and less conspicuous, primarily due to their facades displaying less ornamentation, but still, I have come to believe, should be just as capable of offering the same degree of religious, and spiritual, inspiration.

It shouldn't come as a surprise, due to Crediton being situated in England, that there are numerous pubs here also. Every one appeared to have its own regular clientele. A few were kept in, what I consider, grand condition; their floors swept daily, the glasses on display were polished to a shine, and the chairs available were designed for comfort and ease. There were others, however, that, one might say, were far more ordinary; they were present merely to serve as a form of business, a growth in profits being the goal; hardly places that one could conceive as a "home away from home" for customers.

The main street in Crediton is called, "High", and it stretches from practically one end of the town to the other. It has a sharp dip close to its center, and this is where the town's core is located; all the major stores can be found here; the post office, grocery stores, banks, charity shops, real estate agents, among others. Slightly to the north of this confluence of shops is an open area containing park benches, a small lawn, and beds of flowers, (depending on the time of year). The town's folk had a tendency to congregate here to watch others pass by, chat, or simply savour the opportunity to appreciate the outdoors.

The temperature is mild, relatively speaking, and the weather temperate throughout much of the year. Most of south-western England experiences the same climactic condition as Devon, the county in which Crediton is situated.

When I first arrived here I was amazed, absolutely astounded, by the beauty held within the surrounding countryside. Hills were scattered about, forests covering different proportions of each; sheep, cows, and horses, lazily grazed on the fine, green, pastures that were so full of life, and effervescently robust with the sparkling jewels of nature – so alive, yet able to emit a soothing tranquility.   Somehow, quite often, being able to experience the fullness of what the earth has to offer, can enable a person to feel completely at ease with himself. The eye is able to grasp on to everything that is required to feel content, and satiated.

The train that brought me here would be considered "old" by most in this day and age.   For decades it had carried people over and through the meandering, undulating, landscape of this region.   Each of the passenger cars was "authentic", in the sense that if you wanted to modify the condition of the air in your carriage car, this would necessitate either opening or closing a window varying degrees.   Most of the panelling on the interior of the cars consisted of strips of wood. There are very few trains of this sort still in operation throughout Britain; most today generate their motion by the use of diesel fuel, whereas the type I travelled on emitted puffs of dark smoke from a chimney due to the burning of coal or wood.

Once departing the train at the station it was an easy task to get into town; there was a series of metal steps that lead to the ground level, and from there a narrow paved road led up a small hill, and once reaching the crest, the town would be immediately in front of you.

Crediton retains the splendours of England's glorious past in the bricks and mortar used to build her monuments, homes, stores, and churches.

I decided to come to this town on an impulse.   I remembered well the camping trips my family and I took in this region during my youth. I wanted to rekindle those joyous memories, so they could act as a springboard, enabling me to leap forward, distancing myself from the tumultuous times that had recently passed; many people I had once regarded as friends had betrayed me, as a consequence, I was feeling more alone than I had probably ever felt before.

I passed a few homes until I came across an Inn. It had, no doubt, once served as a home for a family, but had now been turned into a place of temporary refuge, a residence offering warmth, shelter, and a hearty meal. A healthy garden flourished in front of the building, filled with beds of red, and yellow, roses.

I approached the front door, and rapped a metal ring against the hard wood door; thereby announcing my presence to whomever might be inside. Just a few seconds passed before the door was thrust open and inward. A lady stood before me now; her smile and rosy cheeks, presented a warm greeting.

"Hello. Can I help you?"

"Yes, would you happen to have a room available?"

"We have two that have just been vacated. Please step inside. Can I take your bags?"

"That's most kind of you, but I can handle them, thanks."

"Don't be silly, let me take one. It's no bother!"

There was a gentle humour in the way she spoke. I immediately felt welcome. I handed the lighter of the two bags I was carrying to the lady, she quickly latched on to the handle, and then lead me inside by stretching an arm in the direction of the foyer. As soon as I passed her, she shut the door behind me.

"Would you like a room with a single, or a double, bed? I can offer either for the same price; twenty pounds a night, English breakfast included."

"Double sounds fine!"

"Very well then, follow me. It's on this floor, just around the corner to the right. The door's open; make yourself at home."

"Thank you."

"Here's your bag. I'll prepare a drink for you, and something to eat. Would you prefer tea or coffee?"

"Tea sounds great!"

"Get yourself settled, and I'll have it ready in a little while in the "common room", across from your room. By the way, my name is Angie."

"Mine is Henry."

"Nice to meet you; if you wouldn't mind, could you leave some form of I.D. in the "log book"; you'll see it on the small table immediately outside the "common room"; your passport number would be preferable. Is this something you have?"

"Indeed I do; that's no problem."

"Welcome to Crediton. I hope you enjoy your stay."

Our eyes met; I searched into hers, while she, no doubt, was doing the same to me. Angie's age, giving a rough estimate, was late forties, early fifties. For some reason, I was inclined to believe a fair portion of the lines on her face were due to a life of continuous hard work, making her appear older than her actual age; there was a youthful vitality about her, that gave the impression she was younger than the lines, and crevices, and sagging jaw line, indicated. Her straight blond hair was cut short, stretching to just below her ear lobes; if she had kept it any longer, it would have served to diminish the healthy glow somehow written into the chiseled features of her face. The light yellow knitted sweater hugged her small round breasts; that had no real need for a bra to hold them. Her hips were only slightly wider than her waist, presenting sleekness instead of masculinity. When she talked, her voice had a soft, whispery, quality, that was soothing and comforting, much like a mother's.

Once I arrived at the doorway to my room, I was pleased with how large it was. There was an enormous bed in the center of the room. I thought I might have the opportunity to feel somewhat like a king in such luxurious surroundings. I placed my suitcases in front of the chest of draws positioned beside the bed, and then stretched my arms out each side, feeling liberated, and empowered; I'd managed to find a place to rest my head, and revitalize myself, after my wearying journeys, and disappointing engagements with people I'd mistakenly thought were my friends. I looked through the window across from the bed, and took in the glories of England's plush, green, landscape; then, all of a sudden, a voice jolted me from my reverie.

"I have towels here for you. You passed the bathroom; it's at the beginning of the corridor."

"Yes, I saw the sign; thanks"

"Everything's prepared; a selection of newspapers is in the "common room", as well. Enjoy! I hope everything is to your satisfaction?"

"Splendid. Will the room be available for a few days? My intention is to find work in Crediton, and a place to live?"

"Really; you're not a tourist! What's your profession?"

"I'm an artist; I write as well."

"Sure, you can stay as long as you like. I wish you all the best. If there's anything you need, just push the buzzer beside your bed. Breakfast is served at seven-thirty; sausage or bacon?"

"Sausage, please; thank you."

"No problem; bye for now."

When Angie turned around, I noticed that her tight, black, pants, hugged the two well-proportioned cheeks of her rear. There was no doubt in my mind that Angie thought of her body as an asset, and didn't mind putting it on display.

I took my blazer off, and threw it on the bed, then headed to the "common room" to enjoy a hot beverage, some biscuits, and memories of my childhood that I was sure would arise as I sat and stared at the dazzling sights straddling the landscape seen through the room's large window.

Several hours passed, as a reclined in a lavish armchair, reminiscing on the days of my youth, and also pondering what might lay in my future. The only thing I foresaw that might, possibly, hamper the realization of any planned endeavours was the limitation on the funds I had at my disposal. I knew I'd have to execute whatever plans I made quickly, while being as frugal as possibly.

I thought a grand idea would be opening up my own art gallery, a portion of which would act as my studio, and serve as my living quarters as well. I had no shortage of art to sell. I had an enormous portfolio back in Canada that just needed to be brought over.

The following today I put my plan into action, and started looking for a place for my home and business;

fortunately, somehow, everything managed to come together very quickly. Along the way, while gathering all the components I'd need to make my dream come true, I got to know quite a few people that I found quite extraordinary in a great many ways.

The easiest task of all was finding a suitable property. I discovered a vacant place a few blocks above the town's core; it had previously served as a bakery, that managed to thrive, but, I was informed the owners had moved and were now living in New Zealand.

The store had a large window on either side of the front door, stretching from practically the level of the sidewalk to the where the second story began. Real estate agents had informed me two hundred pounds a month was quite reasonable for a property of its size and location; there wasn't any cable included, internet, or even a full bathroom; these were factors that helped explain the low cost.

Once I was able to have a brief conversation with the landlady, I was given assurance the property was mine. All I had to do was wait till the end of the month to sign the lease – by that time I expected to have everything else in place to get my business up and running. I thought "The Art Palace" would be a fitting title for my future establishment. Every morning, I thought to myself, I would pull on a rope that opening velvet curtains that would cover the front windows, revealing my self-created delicacies for all those who might be interested in purchasing, or just taking a closer look.

While I went about making all the necessary arrangements, I managed to meet quite a few people who came across as being pleasant, generous, and kind; each one had his/her eccentricities, thus making conversations with each interesting, and unpredictable; which is something I've always enjoyed.

A distinguished looking lady, with refined manners, ran a "frame shop" in the heart of the town. I arranged to buy, in bulk, some frames from her store, and she immediately offered me a substantial discount if I would simply display her store's catalogue in mine; obviously, this was something I would not find cumbersome, and I right away accepted her offer.

She escorted me to the front door of her store on this occasion, and told me her name was Mary, and presented her card. Just as I was about to leave, she wished me the best of luck, and declared my luck would also be advantageous for her business, and she had the sense we'd make a great "team". She placed a dainty, milky white, thinly boned, hand in mine, as a farewell gesture. A smile covered her face, revealing well-kept teeth; I thought she must be among the few British people left that took the time, and devoted the money, to maintain quality dental work. The wink she gave me, didn't escape my notice either.

With her business card placed securely in my leather wallet, I left her store, certain that in the future I'd find her reliable, responsible, and most co-operative; I saw the possibility of a genuine friendship, as well. Mary was probably the same age as myself, forty four; I couldn't be certain, though, and I wouldn't have dared to ask; being such a "lady", I didn't want to take a chance of offending by asking her age.

I managed to find furnishing; I thought would be suitable for my gallery, from a pawn shop run by an elderly gentleman, who told me his name was, John. He was kind enough to take the time to tell me a bit about the townsfolk, and things I should be cautious about. He had made the determination that more than a small portion of the town's population were ignorant, close minded, fools; however, on the other hand, he professed there was a significant number of art lovers in town and the neighboring villages, and they would be more than delighted about my art gallery being situated in the area.

John, was probably in his mid-seventies, and claimed to have lived in this region for most of his life, and knew well the general likes and dislikes of the population.

He was quite open in declaring that there were a growing number of swindlers, con-artists, and thieves, coming into the area. A large portion, according to his estimation, were immigrants; people who'd essentially come to England with the sole intent to make "easy money"; doing everything possible to make themselves comfortable, while also making themselves "at home". Many hadn't bothered to become citizens, but, regardless, felt entitled to "milk" the system; reaping as many benefits as they possible could, while providing very little, if anything, in return. The type I should watch out for the most, according to John, were the South-Asians, and the worst were the Pakistanis.

The "Pakis", as John called them, had a tendency to label themselves "religious" because they gave themselves the title of being Muslim, but most in town, according to John, did not agree they were actually practicing what they preached; praying to a god named, Allah, five times a day, while facing the direction of

Mecca, didn't necessarily make a person, moral, just, or even the slightest sane. They seemed to have great praise for their homelands, where people were accustomed to blowing up neighbours, and if they were lucky, becoming a martyr by disposing of themselves at the same time.

John's store had many areas that were covered with a thick layer of dust that had probably accumulated over the course of more than a few years. Books, jewels, (of the cheap variety), small appliances, and numerous small pieces of furniture, were scattered throughout all parts of the store. The whole place reminded me of a world within a world, separate from the real world; the type we enjoy escaping to occasionally, in much the same way a novel provides entrance into an alternate domain.

I explained to John my intention of opening up an art gallery in town. There was presently only one in Crediton; it was located just slightly above where I hoped mine would be situated on High Street. The name of the other gallery was, "Gallery 86", which happened to be the street number where it was located. It was run by a group of young people, who had as much imagination, in my opinion, as the name they'd decided would best describe the quality of their merchandise.

I knew, frankly, that I needn't fear the "competition". I'd spoken to a few of the artists one afternoon, only to discover that they were "wanna be artists"; none had much talent, however, they did apparently possess sufficient imagination to believe they actually did. Most had relatives, or friends, who were artists, or claimed to be; maybe they thought that by some process of osmosis they were the same?!

John told me that he was acquainted with these, so called, "artists", and, in his opinion, none were eccentric, or peculiar, but rather out of touch with reality to a starling degree. John informed me that he had ties to the Royal Family, and it was because of his fortuitous heritage that he had managed to develop an appreciation for the Arts, and he had the sense I should be able to develop a thriving art business due to, as he put it, my having "genuine talent".

"Come back here; I'll tell you what you need", he said, with a grin on his face, and a wave of his hand, as he lead me in the direction I needed to follow.

"This, I think, would be perfect. A friend of mine made it himself. It's constructed from an old bed, and a couple of dressers; what do you think? It's a 'one of a kind', if you ask me."

"I agree; I've never seen anything like it. I can picture it in my gallery right now; a throne for patrons to sit on. I'll have the seat, and back cushions, covered with velvet - I think that would be most fitting."

The chair, with its' high back, and wide arm rests, was bulky in appearance, but quite light in weight, due to the materials it was constructed from.

"What's your asking price?"

"For you - don't take that expression the wrong way, I think you're genuinely a nice guy - one hundred pounds."

I wanted to gasp; not due to the price being exorbitant, it wasn't, but due to it evidently being far beyond what I could presently afford. No sound was emitted from my mouth, but there must have been a grimace, or some sign of discomfort, written across my face, because John responded by saying;

"What's wrong? Don't you think it's fair?"

"Oh, I do, it's just..." (I didn't want to reveal the extent to which I was presently constrained by my limited finances), "that I'm being careful right now. You know, there are always unexpected finances that crop up when you first open a business."

"I see; tell you what, I know you love this piece of furniture as much as I do; why don't we make a deal. I have a feeling you're gonna be a repeat customer, and we'll get to know each other better over time, so why don't you pay in installments. Give me twenty pounds now, then come back in a week, and tell me how you can arrange to pay the rest."

I gasped; it had been a long time since anyone had offered me this level of courtesy and respect.

"Do you mean that? I mean, your offer is greatly appreciated. I'm sure once the gallery is set up, I'll be able to pay you back the full amount in no time at all."

"No worries. When would you like it delivered?"

"I'm signing the lease Friday; shortly after that, if possible?"

"No problem at all. I'll give you my card. Give me a call when you get things arranged. I wish you the best of luck; you deserve it!"

John proceeded back to the front counter where he kept his cash box; directly in front of the shop's window facing the street. I walked close behind, while he took the time to remind me of about the town's "foreigners".

"If you trust them, you've only yourself to blame — otherwise, I don't see a problem in you making a success out of your gallery. I'll speak to some people I know, inform them of your whereabouts. You'll have a steady stream of customers in no time at all; try advertising in the newspapers. There are many towns, and villages, nearby that don't have a gallery. I'm sure people will come to town, simply to visit your gallery. What you've done will be of benefit to every shopkeeper in Crediton; I can't thank you enough!"

"Your words are kind."

"They're worthy; not flattering. If there's anything else I can help you with, come in any time."

John stood before the open front door of the store, with his hand extended. I clasped his with mine. I thought I'd made a friend. Many others in town had been similarly cordial and gracious, freely offering advice and support. I thought I'd found myself a home, among people who strived to live their lives in much the same manner I did.

Once I exited the pawn shop, I strolled up High Street toward the core of town. Along the way I passed the old cathedral; the graveyard in front was most remarkable. There couldn't have been a single tombstone less than a century old. Many were smothered with moss, and quite a few were covered with cracks, exposing their age. The script on many had almost entirely disappeared due to weathering. This part of Britain, (much the same as many others on this island), received, relatively speaking, plenty of rain throughout the year.

An old stone path, consisting of chipped, splintered, rocks, led to this intimidating structure's main entrance. There was a tower attached to one side of the steep roof that held a bell which was silent at that time; there was presently no need for an announcement to be heard by those who frequented this place from the surrounding areas.

To me, all this emitted a message every moment of the day, which could be heard by those open, and willing, to receiving. God, in all His glory and might, was protecting you, and me, from the most furious raging storms, but was silent so we wouldn't see or hear Him. We and He will stand the test of time, but only if we choose to make it happen, I thoroughly believe. Many mornings, I was quite sure, a fog, or mist, would mask the presence of these monuments, but the mind, I was definite, could remain certain they were always present.

After staring at this grand spectacle long enough to know that it would be forever retained in my mind, I continued along High Street until I came upon the intersection which included the road that followed the gradual hill leading to the Inn I was staying at. I passed a few people along the way; each offered some form of greeting; a tip of the hat, the wave of the hand, or the greeting, "hello". It was nice to have a sense of belonging; a feeling of connectedness; being a part of something larger than yourself.

The following day I found myself inpatient about meeting the landlady to sign the lease. She had agreed to meet outside my future gallery at seven in the evening. I couldn't wait to officially make the place my own. The future seemed like an ever opening door, containing an endless array of possibilities. All my dreams were coming true; a life in, possibly, at least in my opinion, one of the most beautiful regions of England, being independent, (due to sweat manufactured on my brow), creating works that I hoped would enrich the lives of others for many years to come, and I'd also found that more than just a few of the people I'd come across were incredibly friendly; could I possibly ask for anything more? I knew I shouldn't; I felt like I'd been given too much already!

When I was within approximately a hundred yards of the Inn, I noticed dark clouds collecting above; the threat of rain appeared imminent. I didn't have a rain coat on, nor was I carrying an umbrella; the blazer I was wearing was made of wool, and I didn't want to risk it being ruined by getting drenched in a downpour, so I began to hurry my pace.

Just as I was started feeling confident I might actually beat the looming storm, large, heavy, drops of rain, began tumbling from the sky. I ran the rest of the way, but I still managed to get thoroughly drenched by the time I got to the Inn.

I thought it most peculiar that I then suddenly developed the notion that this was a bad omen of some sort; something bad was about to happen, and in the not so distant future. I had no idea what it could be, or why my mind would formulate such a conception, particularly since so much had been going so incredibly well in Crediton until that time.

I shrugged off this peculiar sense of impending doom by telling myself that I was getting over anxious due to an understandable state of fatigue; there was really nothing to be concerned about, and my imagination was the culprit. Once I unlocked the door to my room, I immediately lay down on my bed. A good nap, I was sure, would set things in order · or would it? I wondered as I quickly drifted off into a deep sleep.

The next day was Friday; "lease day"; today I would be starting a whole new world for myself. I still had a few more things to do, though, before I would be meeting the landlady in the evening; my dream would then become reality.

It then occurred to me that I didn't know the landlady's name; which, I couldn't help but think was rather strange. I'd remembered the names of so many others since I'd been staying at the Inn; why couldn't I remember hers'? I retrieved the card she gave me from my wallet that I'd stashed in the top draw of the dresser beside my bed.

"Francine"; no last name was on the card; apparently, she didn't belong to a real estate firm, which I'd believed was the case for some reason I couldn't quite define or explain. No "title" was used to identify her at all on the card; most unusual, I thought to myself. I decided to quickly shrug off these, what I considered, eerie occurrences, and continue to go about my affairs.

By the time the afternoon hour of four o·clock arrived, I'd successfully completed all my remaining errands; I acquired a landline phone, toiletries, as well as a few small additions to my wardrobe. I also dropped into a hardware store on the outskirts of town, and I was lucky enough to find some paint in a colour I thought would suit the walls and ceiling of "The Art Palace"; lavender, with a touch of purple and red.

I reminded myself that I needed to mention the small repairs that needed to be done; I would also point out to the landlady that both a fire alarm and carbon monoxide detector were missing from the property. A new lock for both the front and back doors would be an absolute necessity as well.

The items I bought during the day were carefully stored in the wardrobe placed in a corner of my room. I informed Angie that I would be leaving the next day, and thanked her for all she'd done.

I still had enough time to spare for a Guinness in a pub at the top of High Street close to where my gallery would be situated. My establishment would be close to its' peak, where it then sloped downward, only to eventually greet the lazy fields that lay across hills, dales, and the valleys containing streams, and the occasional pond containing numerous fish.

I arrived at the store front just before seven, and to my utmost surprise, noticed Francine waiting outside, furiously puffing away on a cigarette. When I was within a few feet of where she was standing, she turned her head in my direction, squinting at me through her dark eyes, and asked: "Henry, is that you?"

Her hair was dishevelled, but the dress suit she wore was formal; it was, however, in need of a cleaning. She had a plump face, much the same as the shape of her body; her waist was the same size as her hips. She had thick calves that pocked out from beneath the dark blue skirt she was wearing. A wondrous sight to behold; I think not; but the key to my future, she indeed was!!

She extended the hand she'd used to hold the cigarette to her lips as a greeting; her smoke was little more than a butt dangling from her lower lip.

As duty called, I shook her hand, then said; "Hello; good to see you."

"Thanks." She then snatched what was little more than a roach from her mouth, and turned around, while dipping a hand into a side pocket of her blazer for the key that would unlock the front door. Once the door was open, Francine flipped the switch just to the right of the door, and all at once the dark vanished, revealing my dream in full colour and bright light; this was the place I'd be living, working, and also selling my art work.

"What do you think? Are you pleased?" Francine asked in a placid, flat, emotionless, voice.

"It's great! Exactly what I'm looking for; this will serve, as I told you over the phone, as both my business, and living quarters."

"Whatever you like; it's your choice." Francine spouted, while looking around at the ceiling, floor, and then the walls.

"I'd just like to say that since this was previously a bakery, the place will need to be fumigated before I move in."

Francine's eyes, most remarkably, began bulging out of their pockets; you'd think I'd just told her the world was about to end! She stood still; seemingly unable to move, as if she were frozen. Her eyes glared at me from their protruding outposts.

After the passage of a few seconds, (though the time, I must admit, seemed much greater), she reached into a pocket of her blazer, and withdrew a small pad and a pen. The cover of the pad was snapped open; she then tapped the tip of the pen on her tongue, before striking it against a page on the pad.

I took this as a sign she was willing to take into account the things that remained to done prior to my moving in. I then listed the items I thought needed attention. She used a grunt as a form of acknowledgment that she'd heard the things I detailed. I couldn't understand, for the life of me, what the big deal was; none of what I was asking her, and was also, by the way, entitled to, would cost all that much.

"Is that all? Anything else you'd like done?" She asked in a softer voice than the one she'd used before.

"No; that's fine. I'm prepared to sign the lease."

"We agreed on three hundred pounds a month; correct?"

"Excuse me! The price we decided on was two hundred pounds; which is fair; considering the location, and the amenities included."

"Fine, O.K.!" Francine snapped.

"I don't have the lease on me. I'll be in Wales this weekend. Give me a call on Sunday; say around 8 pm. We'll arrange a time to meet on Monday, and sign the lease when we meet."

"Great! Thanks very much."

"We should go now; I've got a lot of things to do." Francine said, while placing the palm of her hand on my shoulder, and leading me toward the doorway.

As soon as we both emerged on the sidewalk, rain began to pour from the sky. The darkness of the clouds suspended above had deepened enormously. After Francine locked the front door, she gave me a quick glance, before waving her hand as a farewell gesture, and dashed over to the other side of the street where her car was parked.

Strange, I thought to myself; what was that all about? I shrugged my shoulders, and somehow let the whole bizarre incident wash over me. I then decided to get back to the Inn as quickly as possible, pack my things, and find a cheaper B&B in Exeter, just a short drive away, to save money. I wanted to do all I could to have greater funds at my disposal at the end of the month. My work in Crediton was completed. I was looking forward to a nice, relaxing, weekend, before plunging into my new life as the owner of an art gallery.

Fortunately, once I arrived in Exeter, I found suitable accommodation practically immediately; later, at the designated time, I made a phone call to Francine from a public booth a short distance down the street from where I was staying.

I lifted the receiver, brought it to my ear, dropped the required coins into a slot, and then dialled Francine's number. I waited for her to pick up, which didn't take long; just a couple of rings.

"Yes."

"Hi Francine, Henry here; you told me to call you so we could arrange a time to meet in order to sign the lease."

"Yeh, I've Let the place to someone else."

"What!!"

"Goodbye."

"You fucking bitch!!" I yelled out loud into the night, before slamming down the receiver.

The dream was over; hope had been lost; I had no place to go. I stepped away from the booth, then turned my head to one side, and noticed a man walking toward me, while also experiencing a state of complete disbelief.

"What's up, buddy? You look like you're in a state of distress."

"I just got royally screwed by a landlady. I've been left high and dry."

"Join the club! That's happened to me before. You seem like an O.K. guy; stay at my place a while, until you get yourself situated."

"You mean that?!"

"If I didn't, I wouldn't have said it, and I always mean what I say. We have nothing, if we don't have each other, buddy. Cheer up! Life goes on. My place is just a couple of blocks away; nothing fancy, just a two bedroom."

"God bless you, God bless us one and all. Thank you!!"

"Don't mention it; keep talking like that, though, and I think I might start to blush."

Heaven's Lake

Dancing in the moonlight;
    swaying in the sunlight.

        My heart is filled with songs
    that reach the stars,
    while they skim the waters of the
        nearest ponds.

Like a swan,
the ballerina glides and twirls in the
    wind.
My heart leaps with joy each time I
    hear a melody sing.

She grasps hands with the man that
    completes her soul.
Together they circle each other
till their days grow old.

Dark

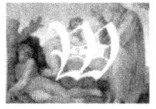hat is the difference
between
good and bad?
By far, it's not hard to say;
  the difference is like
        night and day.

Light opposes dark.
Beware of the night, it is said.
strange things hide, in shadows they bide.

Leave them be, then what you'll see,
will be as it has been;
free.

Light energizes.
Night dulls.
In this lull,
the mind realizes null.

Thus, beware of night; it is where there is
    no light.
It causes fright.
Leave it, or face a fight.

Tomorrow

Day Seven

A New Day

A New Beginning

 fill myself with dismay.
I hurt myself till this very day.
Though lights glow all around;
humorous and bright are these sights that abound.
They surround everything that is dear and kind.

They shine throughout;
from the break of dawn, to the settling of dusk.

They never mind;
they are here to stay,
despite what others might say.

See them in a forest,
or floating on a body of water,
as you stand on a peer.
No matter where you are,
if you search,
you will find them near.

There is beauty in the sight of a leaping fawn.
It carries gentleness so fond;
its joy of nature is there for all to see.

The twinkle in its eye,
shows it knows the reasons why

The Trinity Manifesto; Vol. I

tiny dots glow in the sky.

To life never say bye.
Greet everything with wonderment;
everything is given from Him,
the Most High,
till the day you die.

Don't let fear sweep you away from the
things you love.
Life is only possible,
due to the guiding hand above.

Enjoy this time.
The pleasure lies in not
knowing why or how,
but continuing to say, WOW!!

Nothing in life is more precious than the
chance to exist; to be alive!!

The Goal to Come

 'm passing through a
portal,
I'm very close to where I'm
meant to be.
Everything around is clearer;
what a delight all this is to see!!

The rungs upon the ladder have been many.
So many days have passed in which peace,
there has not been any.

Could it be
that all this was so carefully crafted by
He?
I have an inkling of His nature;
It seems ridiculous to muse the word He,
or equally She;
combined in totality the quantity is
everything.

So many stars,planets orbit around,
galaxies glide here and there,
to and fro,
on and on forever,
this will eventually go.

No beginning, no end.
Light guides, hinders; the messages are
continuous;
but what is the means by which does each
he send?
Is it all an illusion?

The Trinity Manifesto; Vol. I

Is it all contained within?
Remember till the end,
that when it all appears over,
you will appear at a place to begin.

The Lord's Prayer

Our Father
Who art in heaven
Hallowed be thy name.
Thy kingdom come,
Thy will be done
on earth, as it is in heaven.
Give us this day
our daily bread.
And forgive us our trespasses
as we forgive those
who trespass against us
And lead us not into temptation
but deliver us from evil.
For thine is the kingdom
and the power and the glory,
for ever and ever
Amen

The Future

 here it is,
hidden in the distance,
in the dark.
Is it something we should fear?
Or find a lark?

It will always be beyond our reach;
far beyond our grasp.
Why do we bother to ask,
when heaven only knows why we exist at all?

Bask in all glory!
Is he Paul?
Is she Mary?
By God, Christ,
maybe it will lie in our coffin;
a berry,
fallen from a tree,
now lying on the sheltering linen.

Jon & Vangelis
A Play within A Play

You me, me you, when will we be,
Love goes on, no hurry, tell me,
That I know whatever has to be.

Since dreams have their reasons anyway
All the good love stories have their glory
Yours the wind flowing on and on and on
And on and on

Let the winter winds of old
Take the water to the sea
As the man turned into light
Like the forest of the west
They were carrying the fire
Like the boats that sail the waves
In the gardens of belief
Meditate us turn the key
For if troubles share your tears
Rereturning once again and again and again and again
Rereturning once again and again and again and again
For the many to be sure
That's why children seem to know the reason why
True knowledge of believing is believing
I'll find a truth and then believe it till the end
It seems so easy as my life and I begin to know why

Are we to everything a play within a play

What will tomorrow bring?
A golden light and a special dream!

The great thing about the days to come is that they've yet to be written, and it is up to man what will transpire. History has been re-written time and time again, and people have repeated the same follies so many times, they have completely lost their souls.

Life is about struggle and survival, and only those who have managed to retain their essence, their soul, their being, will experience the days to come. Many people might ask; why did it take so long? Why did there have to be so much suffering?

The night is darkest just before dawn.

For the new age to have any hope of being good, every smidgen of what is bad has to be taken away. Picture this statement as follows; the world is a barrel in which are placed apples, and over time, more and more apples became infected – but not all. A few remain healthy; no matter the degree to which those they are in contact with are infected. They remain good by steadfastly adhering to what is *right; which means, following, without hesitation, no matter the circumstance, the Ten Commandments. They are the ones who have earned the right to experience the new age.*

Allow me to provide a vision of how this might appear; the backyard of your home has not been tended to in some while, and as a result, many varieties of weeds have sprouted throughout, making it an unpleasant sight. Just when you think it couldn't get any worse, and every inch is cluttered with these hideous looking weeds, one morning, just after sunrise, you look out a window, and notice all the weeds are gone, every last one, only to reveal a lush, green, lawn you'd entirely forgotten was once there.

Jon Anderson
SONG OF SEVEN

*Haven't you imagination and is it not available
How you can be sooner or later than your thinking.
Haven't you imagination and is it so impossible
That you ask of everything so your eyes can see clearly.*

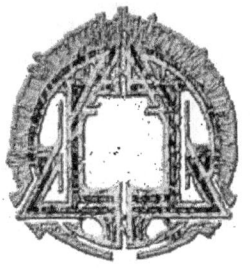

Swami Vivekananda

He is a spirit.
Him the sword cannot pierce him the fire cannot burn him the water
cannot melt him the air cannot dry.
The Hindu believes that every soul is a circle whose circumference is
nowhere, but whose center is located in the body, and that death means the
change of the center from body to body. Not is the soul bound by the
conditions of matter.

Paramahansa Yogananda
Whispers From Eternity
We Demand of Thee as
Thy Children

Thou art our Father.
We are made in Thine image.
We are Thy children.
We neither ask nor pray as beggars,
But demand of Thee, as Thy children,
The gifts of Wisdom, salvation, health, happiness,
And eternal joy.
Whether naughty or good, we are still Thy children, All of us.
Help us to perceive and understand inwardly, Thy Will for us.
Teach us the independent use of our human will,
(since Thou gave it to us freely),
Attuned to Thy wisdom-guided will.

"Daffodils" (1804)

I wander'd lonely as a cloud
That floats on high o'er vales and hills,
When all at once I saw a crowd,
A host, of golden daffodils;
Beside the lake, beneath the trees,
Fluttering and dancing in the breeze
Continuous as the stars that shine
And twinkle on the Milky Way,
They stretch'd in never-ending line
Along the margin of the bay:
Ten thousand saw I at a glance,
Tossing theirs heads in sprightly dance.
The waves beside them danced; but they
Out-did the sparkling waves in glee:
A poet could not be gay,
In such a jocund company:
I gazed--and gazed—but little thought
What wealth the show to me had brought:
For oft, when on couch I lie
In vacant or in pensive mood
They flash upon the inward eye
Which is the bliss of solitude:
And then my heart with pleasure fills,
And dances with the daffodils.

William Wordsworth

William Shakespeare
Sonnet
1

From fairest creatures we desire increase,
That thereby beauty's rose might never die,
But as the riper should by time decrease,
His tender heir might bear his memory;
But thou contracted to thine own bright eyes,
Feed'st thy light's flame with self-substantial fuel,
Making a famine where abundance lies,
Thyself thy foe, to thy sweet self too cruel,
Thou that art now the world's fresh ornament,
And only herald to the gaudy spring,
Within thine own bud buriest thy content,
And, tender churl, mak'st waste in niggarding.
    Pity the world, or else this glutton be,
    To eat the world's due, by the grave and thee.

The Trinity Manifesto; Vol. I

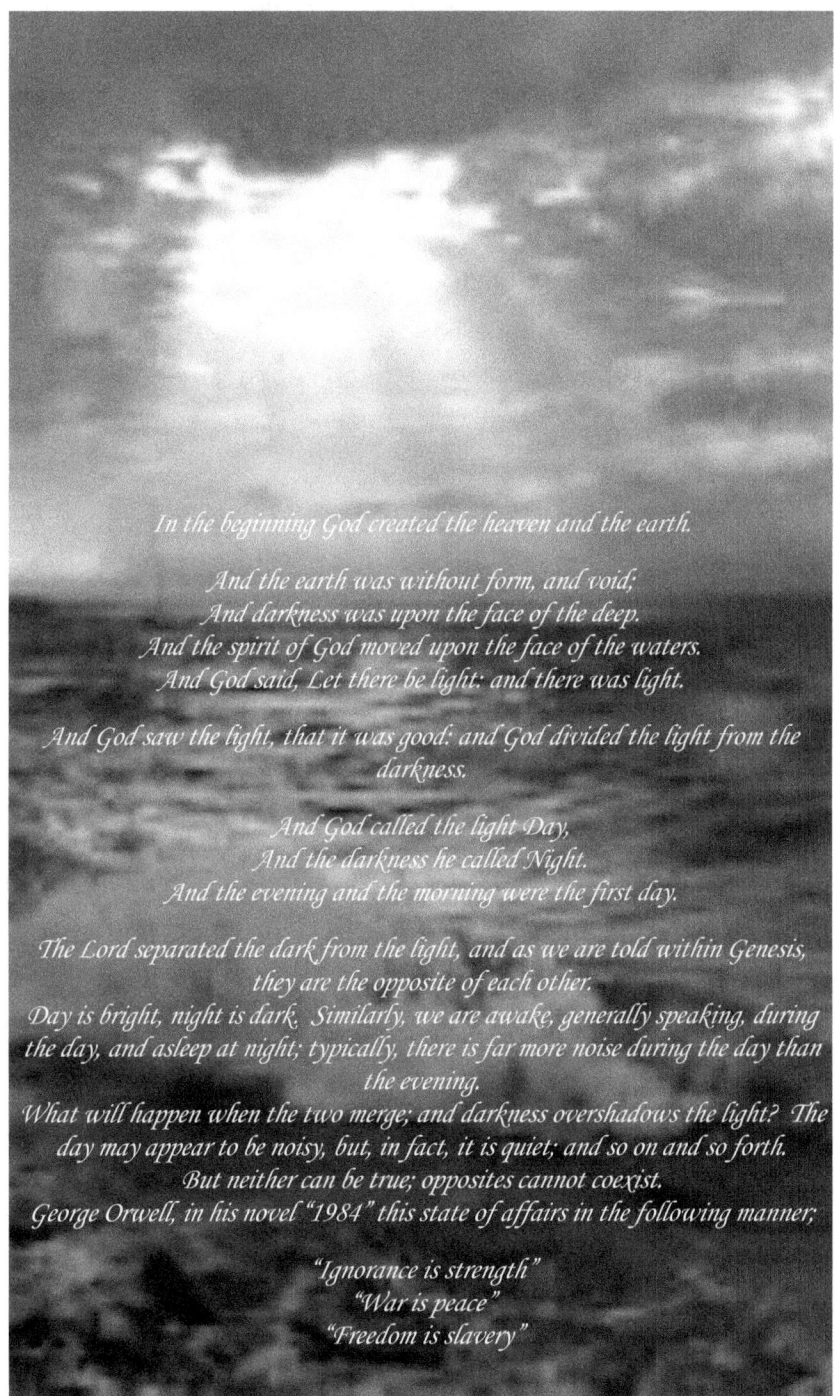

In the beginning God created the heaven and the earth.

And the earth was without form, and void;
And darkness was upon the face of the deep.
And the spirit of God moved upon the face of the waters.
And God said, Let there be light: and there was light.

And God saw the light, that it was good; and God divided the light from the darkness.

And God called the light Day,
And the darkness he called Night.
And the evening and the morning were the first day.

The Lord separated the dark from the light, and as we are told within Genesis, they are the opposite of each other.

Day is bright, night is dark. Similarly, we are awake, generally speaking, during the day, and asleep at night; typically, there is far more noise during the day than the evening.

What will happen when the two merge; and darkness overshadows the light? The day may appear to be noisy, but, in fact, it is quiet; and so on and so forth.

But neither can be true; opposites cannot coexist.

George Orwell, in his novel "1984" this state of affairs in the following manner;

"Ignorance is strength"
"War is peace"
"Freedom is slavery"

Epilogue

In George Orwell's "1984", we are told, "War is peace". If war is peace, then peace is war. They cannot coexist as one, so neither actually exists; rather a story is manufactured to control the masses, that people believe is true, and decide to live by.

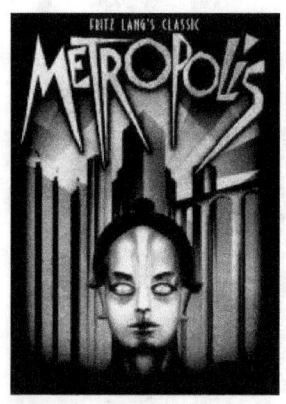

If ignorance is strength, and strength is ignorance, neither actually exists; instead a person is controlled, and led to act in accordance with the desires of others.

Freedom is slavery, slavery is freedom. If you don't work for yourself, or someone else, what is a person doing? Working against himself so that others are able to pull the strings attached to the puppet the person has become. A cage of freedom exists for those who have lost the capacity to reason.

If we wish to be free, and our planet to survive, we have to realize that the truth is the only thing that will keep us alive!

 ow do people perceive God? Generally speaking, in accordance with how they interpret that which they distinguish to be "Holy Scriptures".

The Old Testament within The Bible, for example, is typically perceived by monotheists as both a work of theology, and also a record of historical incidents; in other words, it is construed as being evidence of God choosing to reveal His nature, and how engagements of Mankind correlate with the unfolding of this plan. The primary instrument utilized to accomplish this assignment is His "Chosen People".

History has shown that since the works comprising the Old Testament were concretized, various faiths, belief systems, have been built around them. There is a prevalent belief that the gathering transpired over the course of possibly 11 hundred to 15 hundred years; which would certainly help to explain why there is such a variety of writing styles included, and there are more than a few instances where mythological stories "overlap".

What has happened also, most incredibly, is that acknowledgement of the Jews' role within history has progressively diminished over the passage of each century; ironically, numerous forms of Christianity have been the primary culprit in displacing the status of the "Chosen People"; which is a most peculiar turn of events considering the fact that Jesus Christ is their spokesperson, leader, teacher, rabbi, who proclaimed himself to be a Jew, and apparently, according to versions of the New testament we have today, The Lord was well pleased with him, and instructed others to listen to what he had to say. "Love Is the Nature of Existence" explains how the Jew's managed to build history by fusing ideas, thus facilitating the assemblage of both space and time.

There are, no doubt, many who perceive the God portrayed in the Old Testament as starkly divergent from the God exemplified by Jesus. How is that possible if there is only one God? How can He be so patently quick to display anger, render punishment, and sternly judge, on the one hand, while Jesus portrays his Father as tremendously compassionate, exceptionally forgiving, and spectacularly merciful?

As far as I'm concerned, they are one and the same God, and what is being exposed are different features of His nature. The Old Testament, The Five Books of Moses, focus principally on The Lord's relationship with the "Chosen People"; having said that, consider the saying, "To those whom much is given, much is expected"; is it then remarkable that The Lord severely punishes transgressions of His Laws, and the Jews are expected to follow so many rules; one should consider, as well, that it is customary among schools designed to produce leaders that discipline be emphasized, punishments are harsh, and expectations are greater. The Old Testament could also be viewed as a testament of how crucially important the Jews are within The Lord's scheme of things.

"Love Is the Nature of Existence" details the qualities commonly possessed by those distinguished as Jews, and the conventional ingredients essential to expedite their growth, as well as the conditions required for their incorporation into societies.

Jews appear to spring up during the migration route of the people referred to as Aryans; and there is one strain which has produced a disproportionate number in comparison to their overall population, and that is the Semitic people who for centuries wandered throughout the lands stretching across the Middle East and North Africa.

Having declared the previous, one might understandably ponder how it's possible that the God who supposedly treasures his "Chosen People" so much, has permitted such hardship be placed on them over the course of countless centuries; the "Hebrews" being the most prominent example.

Such a notion, as far as I'm concerned, discloses a muddled conception; what is presented is a "displacement of responsibility". It is The Lord who repeatedly arranged such stupendous contributions be provided to mankind, and it is mankind who failed to acknowledge the value of these bequests, and decided instead to despise, and persecute, those who had only the best intentions.

The finest example of this phenomenon is the execution of approximately 6 million Jews during the reign of the Nazi Party. Hitler, and his henchmen, coordinated a sophisticated propaganda campaign designed to place blame for practically all Germany's ills, shortcomings, and failures, upon its own Jewish population; they became, as a result, convenient "scapegoats" to help explain how Germany managed to suffer the humiliation of having her stature enfeebled on the world stage.

The Allies appeared to have won the War, and stomped out fascism in both Germany and Italy; but then made the tragic mistake of allowing many of Nazi Germany's intelligentsia to reside in their homelands, instead of facing trial for their crimes; thereafter, the knowledge and expertise collected during the reign of the Nazi Party has been used primarily, if not almost exclusively, to secure wealth, rather than insure the preservation of a "master", or "supreme", race which was the professed objective of the Nazi Party.

It was due to a process of "dehumanization" that people decided to participate in the holocaust, among other atrocities, throughout the years 1933 and 1945, (the rise, and the subsequent fall, of the Third Reich) - persuading people to more intently focus on the material, the inanimate, nurtures disconnectedness between people.

This process has been enormously enhanced since the Second World War due to the proliferation of electrical gadgetry, which has now spread to every corner of the

Earth; consequently, an extensive population of people presently believe they can have some sort of "connection" with hundreds of people on Facebook, all the while being immensely concerned with how their persona may, or may not, be perceived by those they consider their admiring fans.

More and more since the Second World War, there has been a shift in First World Countries toward the tearing apart of the family unit. In order for such a plan to be orchestrated, resulting in separating the mother from her child, and at the earliest age possible, it would be essential to impress upon the mother that her behavior was actually beneficial to her child; although, in actuality, her offspring would be denied the opportunity to ever develop into a whole human being.

Many provinces in Canada today are most proud to declare they have full day kindergartens; in most cases, in actual fact, what they are referring to is a Day Care Center; a location where children are kept while parents pursue careers. One should genuinely wonder why such people decide to have children at all. I believe it is fair to say that most are probably inclined to admit they look forward to the time they can have what they regard as an enriching relationship with their child; this will, however, somehow transpire without making any sort of meaningful effort, or a substantial investment of time, in parenting their child; a perception of getting something for nothing, would appear to prevail in circumstances such I have described.

The so called, "Women's Liberation Movement" has done much to instil the idea among women that they are "equal" to men, which conceivably means they have equal opportunity in terms of education, careers, etc.; at the same time the movement repetitively reminds them of how a single mother can be just as capable at rearing a child as two parents; and a man really isn't needed; while also, as bizarre as it sounds, specifying the wonders of such a device as a vibrator, proving, as far as feminists of this kind are concerned, a man isn't necessary at all; which can only be a reflection of the degree of the woman's superficiality.

The sex act is nothing more, therefore, than a pleasurable sensation felt by the woman; seeming to imply that the act of making a "connection" with a male is done with the intent of achieving the same objective. There would not appear to be any shame in exposing a mentality so sick, and depraved.

Why should such an entity (the woman) expect anything more from her offspring than what she has made of herself? How could she even conceive of someone, anyone, having anything greater to offer than what she is able to provide, (the remark is rhetorical).

A key component that enabled the Nazis to obtain power was the burning of books; enormous piles witnessed by hoards of people. Such spectacles were created to not only eliminate any conception German's might have that anybody distinguished as a Jew could provide something of worth, but also instil the perception that anything they were capable of producing would pollute the mind. The overall objective was to insure, as much as possible, that Nazi ideology alone would proliferate among the German people.

It is important to be cognizant that the Women's Liberation Movement has made enormous efforts to suppress the works of both Sigmund Freud and Karl Marx, believing, somehow, their conception of the nature of things opposes, or conflicts, with the picture they wish to convey to the general public. Universities, only thirty years ago, used the works of Freud as a means to introduce students to the other schools of thought in psychology; psychoanalysis symbolized the bedrock upon which all further learning was based.

All these matters help to explain why so many have succumbed to the belief that there is actually a smidgen of validity to "psychiatry"; it is, in fact "pseudo-science nonsense". All the "medications" on the market, (due to their overuse they are "drugs", in the sense they damage the brain), represent just one among various methods presently employed to debilitate the development of consciousness, as well as a person's capacity to reason effectually.

It is heart-breaking to observe the number of people these days that have lost the ability to be cognizant of the manner in which dim, muted, and dark, colors, dampen one's cognitive faculty. If one isn't aware of such being the case, then this is undoubtedly a most reliable indicator that the individual's brain has already been adversely affected to a horrendous extent. I'd like to make an analogy in order to convey what this means.

"Acclimatization" is a physiological adaptive mechanism, it can also, and at the same time, be an indicator that the damage incurred is, possibly, permanent. To provide an example, a person's sense of taste can be dampened by smoking cigarettes. A person can also be rendered entirely devoid of the sense of taste due to a sufficient amount of damage perpetrated upon one's taste buds.

From one generation to the next, particularly since the end of the Second World War, there has been an increase in the extent Man has assaulted himself; according to the depth psychologist, Erich Fromm, the modern age form of evil is disconnectedness between people; the principle instrument used to severe ties has been the T.V. screen

That which, at first, seemed to draw the family together, watching a few shows in the evening in the living room, later, along with other gadgets containing screens, became a devise that hasn't served as a convenience, but quite the contrary, it has damaged society's collective ability to appreciate the environment.

Instead of, to make an analogy, technology making it easier to open one door, so a second can be opened; only door one is opened so more time can be spent cogitating one's belly button. One could call this "human nature", or a propensity to submit to inertia; of course, consistently behaving in such a manner can only become a habit, which will become increasingly ingrained the longer it is practiced.

Man has gone from being a creature that learned to survive horrendous calamities, (at times he was required to spend long stretches of time in pursuit of prey in order to survive), into an entity that refuses to go outside the front door of his home in order to obtain nourishment, but rather decides to feed on members of his own kind; this is, to the best of my knowledge, the greatest taboo. What I have described is how man becomes a brutal savage and resorts to cannibalism in order to sustain himself. How could man stoop so low as to deprive himself of the challenge of becoming a better person.

The Jews

Jews transform people's perception of things; they incorporate elements into societies that weren't there before; they can disassemble whole belief systems, and replace them with something entirely different.

We are here, in the state we are today, due to an inability to recognize the value of the Jew, and his role within society, and, furthermore, the vast scheme of things. He is the protector, the preserver, and also the destroyer – "out with the old, in with the new".

It is quite extraordinary that the greater the numbers of Jews that have been provided to mankind, fewer are the numbers who are able to appreciate their accomplishments. The holocaust was meant to serve as a lesson no one would ever forget, and thus such horrors would never happen again.

"Love Is the Nature of Existence", presents a vision of nature that is entirely the contrary, in most cases the opposite, of how the vast majority conceive their surroundings; but I also explain the path that will lead us toward a sustainable future

Learn to Love

anada has a popular whiskey called, "Canada Club". I believe it was made by Seagram's; but due to its shady, most distasteful, past, it's hard to set boundaries on what it owned, or didn't own; which happened to be run by the infamous Bronfman family. The history of this company, the family, and the product, has much in common with Canada as a whole, and explains, to a large extent, how so many among the population are able to continually spend enormous quantities of money, but at the same time claim to be poor due to having a debt.

When a person immigrates, or lives, in Canada, one is expected to become a member of "Canada's Club"; the objective of this club is to accumulate wealth, so I'll label it a "cult", and because it wishes to keep much of its agenda secret, I could say that it uses the "occult" to achieve its objective.

Most cults, at least the ones that have been studied intensively, conduct their operations in much the same manner as "Canada's Club"; therefore, "Canada's Church" holds members of "Canada's Club". In order for this club to run efficiently, it's important that it not to have a name, or title; say "The Church of Scientology", or "The Mormon Church", and so on and so forth.

Since I have declared that Canada is the home of "Canada's Church Club", it is relevant to ask why anybody would choose to be a member of a cult? Most cults have some sort of "code of silence" regarding what they do, and where their funds come from; and as the saying goes, "If you've done nothing wrong, you've nothing to hide"; furthermore, why would anybody choose to limit, or confine, themselves in any way? When you attach yourself to one thing, you become disengaged from other things; in a sense you are formulating a way of developing of an addiction.

Anybody who's read about cults, (there's no shortage of books on the market), would be familiar with what I've claimed, easily identify one, and stay clear; and it is for that reason that cults strive to keep their members as ignorant as possible, and there are various means that can be used to accomplish this; depriving them of a proper education is a very effective method; "dehumanizing" a person, taking away a conscience, is another way; enfeebling a person somehow, (lack of proper nutrition, insufficient sleep), is another way.

The population of Canada, ("C.C.C."), has a reputation of being apathetic, complacent, lazy, and obese, (sorry, Rob Ford, but you are the poster child for Canada). They are also, for the most part, unaware, much like Rob Ford, of the harm they inflict on others due their stupidity, and ineptitude; even when they are, usually due to being informed by another, it's sad to say, they will tell you they "don't care". On a daily basis I am able to witness "moronic behavior" on display.

I find it quite humorous, in fact, that so many among "Canada's Church Club" actually believe such a thing as an "anger management" course can serve to their benefit, or anybody else's, for that matter. "C.C.C." has a colossal number of corporations that insist their employees whom display displeasure, anger, distaste, and other such unappealing, offensive, forms of behavior, must take such a course. The only thing these corporations are doing, however, is making sure that whatever caused the anger in the first place is not deemed the problem, but rather the problem becomes the person displaying anger, (the exact opposite of what should transpire).

I have often noted that when I express displeasure, or a dislike, regarding the conduct of another, very rarely is there acknowledgment of being at fault, on the contrary, typically a claim is made that there is something faulty about **me**; for example, I could be working at a computer in a library, and the paperwork of the person beside me "drifts" into my workspace; if I were to ask that it be moved, the instantaneous, automatic, response, is usually, "What's your problem!"; a remark that doesn't make the slightest bit of sense; but what's the sense in objecting, or attempting to "communicate", with someone who hasn't a smidgen of common sense.

The objective of the "brain washing" that enables such behavior to take place is so the "work place" is not actually a place where work gets done. Anybody having the intention to get work completed in this "work place", (someone with a "work ethic", and some semblance of a backbone), would indubitably find this unsettling, not just, in the sense that it is more difficult than one expected to accomplish a task at hand, but also because what one expected to be the case, turns out to be entirely different.

To provide another example; when one is studying the environment should be conducive to focusing on one's work, (one would think), and effort is made to minimize distractions. Most evidently this is not the case today within practically all of "Canada's Church Club's" schools, colleges, and universities.

In contrast, I remember well what it was like when I attended kindergarten, and elementary school, in Britain; when someone couldn't keep quiet; he/she might be asked to leave the classroom, go home, go to the principal's office, or maybe stand in a corner and face the wall, and even, if all else failed, have a cloth placed in the mouth, and duct tape over, in order to make the pupil "shut up", and, furthermore, never forget the lesson. I believe such practices would still be in operation today if schools were meant to be places of learning.

The problem, generally speaking, concerning people, is that instead of working to empower themselves, they choose to give into temptation; both the Old and New Testaments provide warnings regarding temptation. In the New Testament it is most often referred to as "Sin", whereas the Old Testament describes it as the breaking of Commandments, not following rules. The problem, as I conceive it, is that little explanation, quite often, is provided as to why something is forbidden; and, most unfortunately, due to a combination of abysmal parenting, and poor schooling, the majority find it difficult to figure out why something is wrong; therefore, people depend on some type of negative repercussion as an indicator of having done something bad.

If a society is designed to insure certain forms of criminal, and aberrant, behavior go unpunished then the inevitable result is a state of anarchy. "Canada's Church Club" makes it difficult, if near impossible, to launch legal cases against doctors and lawyers, for example, among other professionals commonly considered esteemed, which can only have one outcome; while, at the same time, exposing the extent to which the minds of those normally perceived as educated have genuinely been cultivated; within the province of Ontario, for example, doctors are not required to take the Hippocratic oath.

In order to explain the nature of temptation I will use the story of Cain and Abel in The Bible, at the time they are both attempting to impress The Lord, which He admonishes due to it being driven by both vanity, and narcissism.

Love is about being benevolent, charitable, kind, and as generous as one can. If a man can be equated with a tree, then he requires nourishment in order to bear fruit, which will later serve to nourish others. The tree must first occupy itself with the task of acquiring proper, and sufficient, nourishment; even while attending to such an endeavor, it must remember that the act of doing so has a purpose, and that is so fruit has the capacity to grow and enrich others.

Translating my argument in terms of an education, one can have the sense of being grand and wise once it has been acknowledged by someone esteemed that one has grasped key elements of say the works of Voltaire, Plato, Einstein, or Darwin, but then one should use that knowledge, and apply it in a meaningful manner; that is in fact what makes a person wise · being useful.

The biggest problem in the world today is that step two, as one might call it, is rarely realized, and this is typically due to the subject believing he is in possession of all he requires to sustain himself; meaning, in terms of education, to provide an example; prestige, respect, and also a healthy pay cheque.

He may justify his actions in terms of money, i.e.; "I paid for my education, thus, I am entitled to do whatever I please with the education I acquired". Such a person has become so attached to the object, the idea, of "money", (an inanimate object), he has entirely forgotten his humanity, and, as a consequence, that he has a part, plays a role, within an ecological system; quite obviously, for it to be sustainable, that which is taken, must be replaced; I call this, simply put, "The law of Reciprocity".

In order for a person to behave, and think, in such a manner, a conscience, a "superego", is required; the more we practice morality, greater is our connection, understanding, and appreciation, of The Source, God, the ocean of life, the cosmological ecological system; whatever one wishes to call the grand scheme of things.

Animals, as zoologists inform us, live in harmony with their surroundings, which insures the sustainability of an ecological system. They eat, and drink, what they require, and when needed: that is one way of explaining the reason why animals, when healthy, do not perform acts of cruelty, perform torturous deeds; beyond being distasteful, animals do not waste resources.

Animals and humans, as I have detailed, are supposed to collaborate their behavior in order to sustain the environment. A complication is present, however, that can easily, and quickly, dismantle an environment; unlike animals, people are given entrance to a gargantuan reserve of energy; The Source, cosmic consciousness, the well spring from which all life stems.

Man is also given free choice and free will, which means nothing else than the capacity to develop a faculty of reason. As is the case with any other type of resource, man decides whether it is used wisely or not; the greater the mind is cultivated, closer, wider, and greater, is his connection to the source - each increase is earned.

What The Lord determined He would do in order to assist man to join Him, become entirely Spirit, one and the same as Himself, was provide mankind, by way of the Jews, tools to cultivate the mind; a concert pianist, for example, may use the works composed by J.S. Bach to better his skills.

The problem that has developed time and time again throughout history is that man misuses the gifts The Lord so generously extends; he does this by deciding to give into temptation. If a person is moral, has a conscience, he will use a resource to do what is right, that which is good, and will, as a consequence, help sustain an ecological system, rather than compromise its existence.

In order to improve on something it must be challenged, much like climbing to the top of a mountain;

each increase in altitude requires an expenditure of energy; of course, we should do whatever we can to facilitate such a journey. If I wish to be a world class 100 meter sprinter, for example, I would, of course, do whatever I could to keep my body as healthy, and strong, as possible.

Only by improving oneself, by searching, reaching, for something higher, or, to use eastern expressions, aspiring to achieve self-realization, can one be in harmony, in tune, with an ecological system.

With an expansion of one's consciousness, one will also drift into larger, possibly different, ecological systems; that is why it is commonly believed that people such as Moses, Socrates, William Shakespeare, Beethoven, and Jesus Christ, managed to achieve a state of consciousness separate from the common man of his time. To make a comparison; when one achieves an honorary undergraduate degree, and enters a Master's program, one no longer claims to be an undergraduate student. One's capacity to be altruistic goes hand in hand with the development of the self. Another way of expressing this is by saying that one's ability to appreciate the nature of love increases in relation to the extent a man practices being good.

What happens when power falls into the wrong hands, i.e., those who are not reaching toward the good, but are instead leaning toward the dark, or have a tendency to give into temptation, and, thus do the opposite of love? They, inevitably, destroy instead of create, and one is able to identify such types by the magnitude of their narcissistic temperament. They not only harm themselves, but their surroundings as well;

the greater the power provided, so too is the potential for harm to be done. That is why so many today do not recognize technology as our greatest blessing, but rather our worst curse. It is a well-known fact, for example, that Albert Einstein enormously regretted the creation of the atom bomb, knowing, full well, because of the immense power it held, the magnitude of destruction it could cause if it fell into the wrong hands.

Our world has been following a downward spiraling course since the Second World War, and this has definitely been due to the misuse of information; unbeknownst to the general public, this has actually been our greatest enemy; we have not just compromised the survival of the human species, but also the Earth's capacity to sustain life on its surface.

What we now call, "modern psychology", arose during the late Nineteenth Century; Sigmund Freud's landmark book, "The Interpretation of Dreams", was published in 1900; shortly after other names appeared who managed to make enormous contributions to the field in their own "individual" way; Carl Gustav Jung, Alfred Adler, Abraham Maslow, and Carl Rogers, are notable examples.

Psychology is commonly conceived as the last of the sciences to develop. It can be considered a science, identical to both biology and chemistry, if one explores the manner in which data is collected, and then formulates a theory to explain, for example, how, and why, certain patterns appear within information gathered; ironically, what could have served as mankind's greatest treasure, has turned out to be the exact opposite; our worst, and deadliest, foe.

Shortly after World War II, the "Monolith" started collecting information about the behavior of people around the world, among other things, in order to find a means to acquire wealth, while exerting themselves as little as possible.

This would mean, to make an analogy, that instead of acquiring sufficient capital to invest in the construction of a factory, and employ people to work in it, and then keep much of the profits, the eventual goal was to have others do all these things, while you, "a member of the Monolith", manage to keep a share of the profits.

The people responsible for coordinated this scheme were the worst form of narcissists, and, quite obviously, anybody who was a participant in this scheme had to have been a savage, by definition; which would explain why there was such a massive number involved in the design and implementation of this plan; their individual brains being so small, one would require a microscope to examine it.

The finest example in existence today of the degree to which this scheme has been a success is Canada, ("C.C.C."). Anybody can pick up one of the "classic works" on "cults" and learn how the Monolith managed to make people behave in accordance with their wishes; all the popularly recognized cults operate the same way.

If anybody is wondering, at this juncture, why the "Christian" faith has so many "Churches"; it's because they are actually cults, and, thus, the furthest article from the top of their agenda is the promotion of the Ten Commandments. Any faith, religion, that discourages questioning, could in no way enhance a person's capacity to reason, and, therefore would not be able to enhance a person ability to connect with The Source; I can, therefore, label all "fundamentalist" faiths as not being religions.

Canada is not a sovereign country in the sense it has laws and a government; it is no different from the innumerable crack pot institutions cropping up all over the place, striving to hide their funds, and what they do to acquire them.

People are willing to invest in these sorts of establishments because each pretends to be able to make a person better, somehow healthier, and are also involved in some sort of "altruistic mission". Canada, "Canada's Church Club", is an enormous country with vast resources, which translates into power. It is enormously wealthy, but appears capable of only misusing whatever resources it has.

It is common for cults to try and trap those who are suffering, or going through some sort of personal turmoil; a person seeking comfort, security, and friendship; that is the primary reason why "Canada's Church Club" invites refugees from around the world to immigrate to this country, and why it continually tries to instil fear and doubt within the population at home. It is hard to find someone, for example, who doesn't believe there has been a recession in this country over the last two decades.

A common method used to control a person is to keep him ignorant, and also provide a false sense of security; that way a person is discouraged from questioning whatever it is they are being told. Individuality within a cult is admonished, because such a thing would necessarily comprise being creative, and original, which requires cognitive activity, and that is why "homogeneity" is encouraged.

The amount of exertion devoted to this task is in proportion to the foreseen strength, or threat posed, of the adversary; it definitely doesn't take much, I must say, to influence the lazy, gluttons, belonging to "Canada's Church Club".

Much like any other cult it has different departments that have a specific, or specialized, role to play; two notable, and obvious, factions within the "C.C.C." are "The Black Cult", and the "Feminist Cult"; anybody involved in politics, directly or indirectly, actually has a job with the "House of lies", also known as, "The Department of Truth".

"Canada's Church Club", much the same as all other cults, attempts to have, what it considers to be, a charismatic spokesperson; evidently, at this time the best "C.C.C." can do is Mr. Stephen Harper; I wouldn't be at all that surprised, however, if behind closed doors he's prone to behave in much the same manner as "C.C.C." 's other star attraction, Mr. Rob Ford.

As proof of the extent of this cult's success is the "C.C.C." debt, and that what it exports doesn't even remotely compare in value to what it imports; excluding Canada's "Missionary" missions abroad, such as Afghanistan, for example; where "C.C.C." placed poorly trained, and ill equipped, soldiers. The defense minister recently admitted that this was the case; but only after the war was over!! For some bizarre reason many members of "C.C.C." had "Support Our Troops" stickers on the bumpers of their cars; I'd like to know if anybody found a way to support the troops, (of course we already know the truth). The people who form the members of the "C.C.C." are no different from the state; they are the state; they are, "Canada's Church Club".

The universities in Canada only require two things from their students; 1) they attend a sufficient number of classes, and, 2) pay for their courses. That is why the "students" that come to the campus grounds of any one of the universities in "C.C.C." don't actually do any work; they sit, talk, drink coffee, watch shows on their computers; and make sure those who are actually "good", find it as difficult as possible to get work done. Each and every one could educate himself if he chose, but that doesn't seem sensible; after all, he already has, or so he believes, everything he needs.

The young people of today were brought up by parents who were much the same, and that is why inanimate objects became their friends, instead of people.

Cults have to make sure people don't question what they are being told, (blind obedience is the optimal condition), in order to limit their access to "outsiders", therefore, hindering their capacity to accumulate information. Few members of "C.C.C." have an interest in anything beyond the scope of their own lives.

We must, right away, as a species, cease our mindlessness, and work on preserving the planet; which means loving one another; but first of all one must learn to love oneself. Canadians may believe this means going to the mall, and engaging in retail therapy, but I actually mean stepping toward the light, and correspondingly, away from the dark.

The Fall and Rise of Human Civilization

he truth is being hidden by a lie. The lie is used to acquire wealth. The level of exertion devoted to the manufacture of the lie is proportionate to the conceived threat of the truth being exposed.

The lie can be equated with the Dark. What is the "Dark"? How is it different from "Light"?

Creation stems from light, which is good. Love, as I describe it in "Love Is the Nature of Existence", is good, and it is for that reason it has the capacity to create. Creation is good, because it loves to create.

I will describe the nature of the Dark by illustrating the manner in which it infiltrates a person's life, then festers until it is able to entirely overwhelm a person, taking away a person's identity, so all that remains is the ability to destroy; oneself, then eventually all one comes in contact with; all the while having the capacity to experience pleasure in being able to induce suffering, pain, sorrow, and hardship.

Good, love, light, on the other hand, nourishes; it creates something advantageous for others. Parents should function in much the same way, and labor to instill qualities within their children that will enable them to one day be productive members of society.

If parents are earnest in their quest to achieve this objective, they will as well openly reveal their weaknesses; quite obviously to insure their offspring understand that if they fall short of the standards they expect of themselves and others, this is not due to being underhanded, or deceitful.

Love, is honest, upfront, creative, and supportive. In contrast, Dark is dishonest, underhanded, devious, violent, and destructive. Someone who's genuinely creative has the capacity to manufacture something new, original, and unique. The Dark, typically, likes to portray itself in a similar manner, but it is only able to do such by stealing, or plagiarizing, the works of others.

What has most notably become a widely prevalent trait within the Arts today is that which can be labelled as "serialization"; to provide an example, a chain of movies based on the same kernel of an idea. There are many popular authors today that function in much the same way; such spectacles could also be considered as the reason why our world is in such a pitiful state.

For the past several decades mankind has failed to provide a fresh new seed; one able to sprout the answers humanity requires to solve the ongoing, worsening, problems plaguing our world.

It is important to keep in mind, however, that if we conceive The Lord as the ruler of all, He must have decided, given all His wisdom, that such a state of affairs would serve to better mankind as a whole; therefore, it can be concluded that the suffering, pain, and hardship, experienced by so many must be the consequence of a heinous, deplorable, despicable, deed; so enormous in scope, one might say, that it is beyond quantification.

Contrary to the conception held by so many today, suffering for the misdeeds one has perpetrated has throughout history, and in all quadrants of the world, with very few, and minor, exceptions, been considered the keystone, the bedrock, upon which any hope of transforming a person's behavior is based; the more severe the crime, greater the penalty.

The Lord, in all His wisdom, decided to deny mankind His greatest treasure for two complete generations. I cannot imagine a more severe sentence. To make an analogy; picture a man brought to the very brink of starvation before being presented a crumb than can do little more than whet the appetite.

The Lord withdrew the most crucial ingredient required for any civilization to survive – the Jew.

Ever since the last blessed our planet, mankind has relentlessly, and persistently, squandered, misused, and abused, knowledge that has been granted. The last giant among the physicists was, without a shadow of a doubt, Albert Einstein, who memorably gave warnings in regard to the threat nuclear technology posed to the survival of our planet; till this day it continues to be used by various countries as a device to achieve a goal with the mindset that the end justifies the means.

So many people, in so many ways, have expressed their deep despondency regarding the state of the world, and there being any chance of things getting better; and for some reason can, as well, fathom things getting worse than they presently stand. That is really quite impossible because it is the lie that is evil and destroys, and a lie can be either completely concealed or exposed.

When people live a lie every moment of the day, that represents the furthest extent it can grow; such has already transpired in the world, and at that time, one would presume our punishment should be over, and The Lord will then liberate Jews from the heavens so humanity once again has the capacity to grow, love, and learn; and hopefully, appreciate to a degree never before in existence, what was lost, stripped from their possession.

The Dark found its way into people lives by people becoming less and less conscious and aware of their surroundings. Another way of expresses this is by making the assertion that people gave into temptation, and, thus, weakened themselves, and the Dark chose such a vulnerable time to surge into their life - its desire is for you.

Shortly after the Second World War the "Cold War" began, and the "Iron Curtain", as Winston Churchill called it, was erected. Contrary to popular belief, communism, in the Marxist sense, was not the enemy, or foe, of the Allies, the "civilized world", but rather Josef Stalin, and "Stalinism".

Josef Stalin believed "communism" could exist in a single country, and, thus, did not require a global presence in order to survive, which was the form in which both Lenin and Trotsky believed it could only manage to sustain itself.

The goal of communism, simply put, is a classless society; one that exercises equality for all; a mandatory respect for the Rights of each and every person. The fashion in which it believes this can be made possible is by curtailing the consumption of resources.

Capitalism is a free enterprise system that can only be maintained when boundaries, borders, are acknowledged, which means, at the very least, that it has to be "nationalistic"; which also enables the development of a culture. Adam Smith's three rules for limiting corruption are compulsory in insuring a sustainable capitalistic economic system.

History has shown, quite obviously, that Adam Smith's rules have been increasingly broken since the Second World War. Technology, for the most part, has been used primarily to increase the comfort, and convenience, level, of those residing in the First World; all the while an increasing number of products have been processed in the Third World.

The disparity in wealth that exists between these two Worlds has steadily grown since the fall of the Third Reich, which was supposed to bring an end to tyranny, and brutality, of the sort that had never been recorded prior to the Nazi Party coming to power. Is this the case? If one examines the nature of existence, and what is required for it to be sustainable, then the answer is, evidently, **NO**!

We are, by nature, producers, creative beings; one way of expressing this is as The Bible does; man should toil till the end of his days; this is good. Evil, on the other hand, consumes, and much the same as any other behavioral pattern, it will become more pronounced over time. Evil, hence, is more prevalent in the First World, than the Third World; the worst forms of brutality, as a consequence, will transpire in these countries.

Canada is the world's champion consumer society. The people, as a consequence, are more disconnected, desensitized, and indifferent, to the plight of their fellow man, than anywhere else in this world.

If one isn't producing, one must steal in order to sustain a life; consumerism being an entropic force, evil will proliferate over time, until it achieves an absolute form; people will then have no capacity to restrain their actions, and will, thus, do anything, as long as there is an impression the act will exclude any form of recrimination.

Evidently, to be comfortable behaving as such a manner a conscience would have to be absent. Those who set the scheme specified in motion had to first attack its greatest enemy, a person's superego, which is also the gateway leading to the resource that makes us different from all other animals on the surface of this planet. The execution of the plan began shortly after the First World War

In the year 1920, women "got the vote" in the U.S, and ever since there has been a slide toward women becoming more and more consumerist in their ways, and, at the same time, neglecting their children in an increasingly pronounced fashion; throwing gadgets at them as a means to fill their time, and, as a result, compromising their ability to cultivate their minds. It is a sad, and pitiful, sight to see so many who have already reached so called "adulthood", but manage to consume vast quantities of time playing video games on buses, trains, and cars, and in shopping malls, food courts, and office buildings.

Universities today are filled with those whose sole aim is to obtain a piece of paper allowing them the opportunity to acquire a pay cheque; they are, most regretfully, at the same time thoroughly unequipped to make any sort of meaningful contribution to the well-being of others. The finest post-secondary campuses, containing the most remarkable libraries, are, to a spectacular extent, wasted.

If someone should come along who actually has something to offer, the university will use every measure, and resource, at its disposal to steal it; hence, eliminating any hope of the extraordinary person acquiring a career of worth in the future; therefore, the least gifted is far more likely to graduate from a post-secondary institution than someone of substance.

The human, in such a circumstance, is viewed solely in terms of his monetary value; he is a resource, instead of being treasured for his ability to produce a resource; such is how people view each other in a consumer society. The only thing of value within an exchange of information is that which is foreseen to have the capacity to enrich another; therefore, no genuine human contact, connectedness, is transpiring. The person is always preoccupied with the act of fulfilling itself, enhancing its ability to consume; that is why lives are lost in a country such as Canada in order to feed the consumerist lifestyles of its population, and there is no guilt, shame, or remorse, attached to such barbarous deeds – it is simply business as usual, nothing personal.

When one lives in a shelter, for example, in Canada, one is denied any paper record, document, as proof of residing there; which means the occupant is viewed as a commodity, and every possession of value belonging to that person will be stolen; by force if necessary, and at the very first opportunity; and the police will be present to insure there is no legal consequence attached to such a horrendous travesty of justice.

The youth of today cannot change the world; make it better, in any way. They are products created by our sick society, and their parents who, for all intents and purposes, abandoned them while seeking to acquire riches in order to live the lifestyle of their choice.

The Lord, thank goodness, will again offer His chosen as compensation, and we will be saved from ourselves; and the chance for every species on this planet to be annihilated will no longer be a possibility.

GIANTS

Will descend
From the heavens,

And walk the Earth
As they did in Ancient times,
And have many times
Before and
Since.

Mayan Mind Set

Hidden within the deep forest
were Mayan temples
They praised many gods,
most of all the Sun.

    Sacrifices were made
to insure that all would be made more
    abundant.
Hope sprang forth,
excluding the need to feel glum.
Though serious were their various
    endeavours;
practically all made time to enjoy
    themselves,
to instill a sense that life was fun.

Dancing, singing, praying, chanting,
    rhyming, speculating;
continually immersed in the inspiring quest
    to reach truth.
Never content to feel settled,
till all that had been said was done.

The Mystic

The mystic sees beyond.
By fighting for what is right,
they make themselves akin to light.
How they must be filled with delight!
Wondrous are the stories they tell.
Some can resound in one's mind like a bell.

Always beware of those who have
        something to sell,
they are the ones that will send you to hell!

Why is it they number so few?
There are, after all, so many that sit in a
        pew.
Answer this question, I cannot, because,
I simply, don't have a clue.

They do more for us than we recognize,
or presently realize.
They teach, inspire, guide;
so many things with which we should
        better familiarize,
and disdain the act to disguise.
These great things they have said
are incomparably wise.

Listen when they speak.
In time the heavens you will be given a
        peek.
That is the only thing we should strive to
        seek.

Love is
The Father
The Word is the Son
Time is the Holy Ghost

TRINITY

The Father, the Son
the Holy
Ghost

May peace return among men
Co-operation unite them
Friendship bind them
Love rule them
Justice prevail among them
Self-control strengthen them
Righteousness exalt them
Service enoble them
Brotherhood enfold them
The past be forgiven them
The future be sanctified for them.

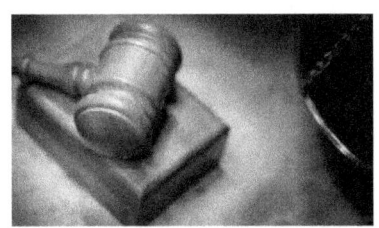

MAN & NATURE

The idea, concept, word, "religion", is an expression of Man's appreciation and understanding of the nature of things; that he is related to, and dependent on, powers in nature and society.

Ancient man, in many regards, appears to have been far more religious than most in our present world. When Cro-Magnon man emerged, some 25,000 years ago, the Earth's climate was milder, and life was far less hazardous than it had been for Neanderthal man, (both are members of the species Homo sapiens), and their finest cultural achievement was art work derived from painting and modelling.

They believed, much as so called "primitive" peoples do today, that an image, or picture, can be a magical substitute for the object it represents; it could be subjected to his influence and obtain power.

Many of these pieces of art included pictures of animals, and some had human faces; representative of their belief that there was a spiritual kinship between animals and people, and members of the wild kingdom could serve as their protectors; "guardian angels", in a sense.

RELIGION & NATURE

Religious thought has evolved over the centuries, more in some parts of the world than others, and every belief system has been an attempt by man to make full use of his life by reminding him of where he belongs within the "vaster" scheme of things, thereby enabling him to more proficiently utilize resources, all the while increasing his sense of security and comfort.

Ancient tribes practiced what some call, "totemism"; which is a belief that each class of animal, plant, and inanimate object, has its place within the food supply; or as we would otherwise commonly call it today, the Earth's ecological system.

Ancient people's understood that their supply of food was dependant on their being a plentiful supply of the other elements that go into the making of food; therefore, they performed ceremonies, and practiced rituals, in praise of the Earth, and made sure, as much as possible, that what was taken from the Earth was replaced; that way all animals and plants would increase and be abundant.

They were connected to the "Life Force", as I would phrase it. Erich Fromm, the neo-Freudian, personality theorist, would label this as a "syndrome of growth", or biophilia.

About the Author

The author was given the name, Nigel, at birth, a very common name in Britain, and seven days later conforming to Jewish custom, a circumcision ceremony was performed and he was given both the Hebrew name Tovia and the Yiddish equivalent Tevia, both names imply the blessings and goodness that God bestows. In later years whilst living in Israel he adopted the Hebrew name Eitan, which implies stoicism and impetuousness.

All these terms, expressions, are a reflection of his nature. He has depth and complexity, but can display banality, depending on his mood, or the time of day.

Due to fate, circumstance, destiny, (whatever term deemed appropriate), over recent years he has not just engaged in a battle with himself in order to become fully actualized, but also a nation called, Canada.

He admits that he neither wanted, nor desired, many things that have encroached on the lifestyle he sought to acquire for himself, but by conquering each obstacle placed in his path, he managed to realize himself in a span of time previously never imagined possible, and as a consequence, figured out why the world is in the state it is now.

His life has been filled with great struggles, from early childhood onward, and the education he has provided himself is primarily the result of questioning, wanting to better understand, why people behave the way they do, and how certain circumstances arise.

Time, history, existence, can be viewed as a story; a story is written with words, and the combination, synthesis, of these words formulates ideas. A story concludes when enough ideas have been coordinated to reveal the design, purpose, and reasoning, behind a plot.

If a new beginning is upon us, and time can be contracted by the formulation of ideas, and Nigel Shindler's book is seen as an amalgamation of the primary concepts that have formulated the history of human civilization; it is mankind alone that is responsible for this occurrence.

The author was recently awarded a Ph.D. in psychology by Ashley University, (an internationally accredited online university), on the basis of an earlier edition of "Love Is the Nature of Existence".

The Trinity Manifesto

What makes a person human? That is the question.
We now live in a world of extremes; some labour too hard, while others seek to continually ease their woes at an enormous cost to others, and also themselves.

Dr. Rollo May wrote a book entitled "The Meaning of Anxiety", in which he challenged the belief that mental health is derived from living without anxiety, but rather asserts it is essential to the human condition; confronting anxiety can relieve boredom, sharpen sensitivity, and, actually creates the tension necessary to preserve human existence.

Following the Second World War humanity, understandably, sought relief from the horrors, carnage, and suffering, that had taken place, as well as the decades leading up to it; never mind the First World War, (1914-1918). The problem is that humanity never brought to an end this search to relieve hardship.

With each passing decade "convenience products", and "consumer goods", in increasing numbers have seeped into the lives of those who inhabit the "First World", while the anguish of those residing in the "Third World" has intensified, while they are forced to labour in order to fulfill the wants, needs, and desires, of those already over-saturated in material wealth; and, ironically, aren't even close to realizing this is the case – our environment has had to bear the strain of this burden.

How can this cycle of madness be brought to an end? "The Trinity Manifesto" explains that the answer lies in remembering what makes us human, and how the completion of this accomplishment leads to the whole, the Truth, Self-realization, God – the big picture.

Being human means to behave in a humane manner; one takes care of oneself, while also taking care of others. We each grow by making connections with others, then, eventually, the great beyond.

People, however, have followed the opposite course, and as a consequence dissolution, fragmentation, and disintegration, has spread, and at the cost of losing the most crucial ingredient that makes us human; our soul.

A confluence of entropic forces within all of mankind's major civilizations, since the beginning of recorded history, has led to the state we are in now; this hasn't happened by accident, but rather design, divine in origin.

The Holy Ghost is the water of life that
nourishes every living thing. It is life, love, giving, truth;
everything that is you.

From a word stemmed life; an ever renewing life force. It
endlessly evolves, while using itself as a resource to churn
the cycle of life.

History involves pivotal moments in time that determine
the events to follow. For life to continue, the new must be
generated from the old, and preserved for a time so the
chain of events can continue once again.

Creation is an act of love; it is perfect, whole, and complete;
the same as the entity from which it came,
and is also a part of.
Love is nature, enfolding itself within
the elapsing of time.

Love Is the Nature of Existence

Love Is the Nature of Existence

VOLUME
I

The Trinity
Manifesto

Love Is the Nature of Existence

VOLUME
II

Love is The Word and the
Time is Now

Love Is the Nature of Existence

VOLUME
III

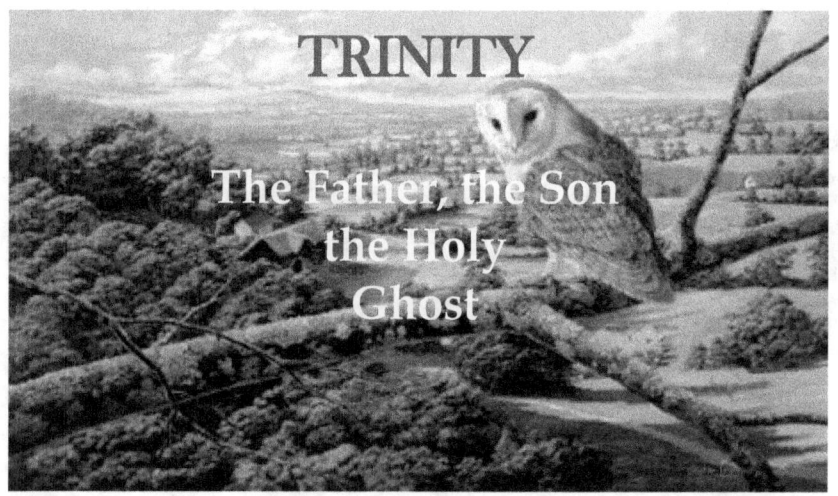

TRINITY

The Father, the Son
the Holy
Ghost

Love Is the Nature of Existence

VOLUME
IV

THE
CREATOR

COMING SOON

The Boy and the Tower

The
Memoirs of
Nigel Shindler

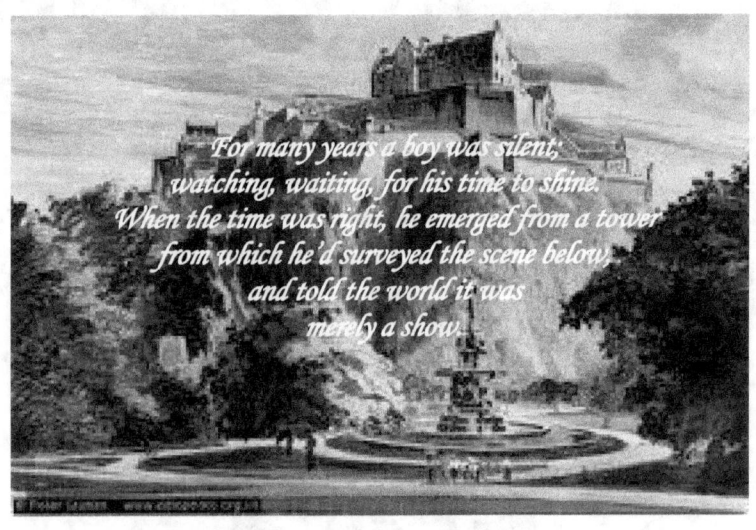

For many years a boy was silent,
watching, waiting, for his time to shine.
When the time was right, he emerged from a tower
from which he'd surveyed the scene below,
and told the world it was
merely a show.

COMING SOON IN
HARDCOVER, PAPERBACK, AND EBOOK

A Boy and the Tower

The boy stood
in front of the tower,
all alone,
he could feel the
power within;
   then wondered;
      where everyone else was?
Who cares, he thought, after all, I'm the
   boss.

There is a world
filled with everything you could possibly
   need.
You are a seed,
that grows and grows,
then one day, who knows, maybe you'll
   know it all,
then, in totality, you'll be whole, complete,
at the same time, unique;
you!

Others are far, but you don't need them.
You have you. All you need.
There are you in the shadow, in the light;
awake at dawn and night.
Everything is awakened to the
surroundings you have around you.

The beauty of it all

dances with sweet delight.
On angel's feet, you take to flight.
There it is above in heaven;
bright light!
There is never a fallen night
It's perfect, it's right.
Everything is good once again,
there is no pain, nothing more to gain.

You had it all in the beginning.
Only at the end
did you realize this.
No longer
is there a hiss.
The serpent has
disappeared;
all that is left
is a kiss

The Poet

*W*hat is a poet?
Life offers him
so many pleasures,
he often dances with joy.
Requests are made, that
on his journeys others join;
Sailors, ahoy!

Months and years are filled with play.
Each object he sees as a toy,
this occurs no matter the day.

Magical are the pulsating
visions and stories present in his mind.
Each one deserves an embrace.
The urge to display these wonders means
they can often be put down in haste.
Later the search for perfection sets in;
the quest shall begin to let each of heaven's
angels
rest on the head of a pin.

Haunted by sights of things past,
he displaces with a rose,
on whose petals tears of rain roll.
Alas, each he greets with courage he knows
will last.

Inspiration arises with the sound of
trumpets blaring.

The Trinity Manifesto; Vol. I

Bursts of thunder announce their call.
They can live in dungeons, vast forests, or
    a mountain top,
no matter where, there he will find a
    fountain.
Gates will open, ideas can then flow.
Precious are these things,
their light is so sweet, they often glow.

Their hearts, and minds,
soar on the wings of elegant, delicate,
    birds.
Free, they always desire to be.
Never shall one belong to a herd.

They transport themselves.
Around the globe they go.
Where have all the great ones gone?
I don't know.

My earliest memories take place in the town of Reading, situated just west of London, England.

My family lived in a two story house in a, as I would put it, comfortable residential district; meaning, the people were far from struggling to get by, but rather had the time and means to enjoy recreational activities on a regular basis.

My family was no different, and I keenly recall excursions made several times a year to Liverpool, where my grandmother and many of my other relations lived.

The closest ties I would make throughout much of my life would not be among my neighbors, classmates, or any group I joined, but rather relations on my father's side of the family, and the kids that lived in my grandmother's neighborhood.

I recall my life in Reading as being a rather solitary existence. For the most part I played alone, and when I was at home I kept to myself, enjoying my own company, having limited contact with my immediate family members. This was a pattern that continued throughout much of my life, for various reasons, the primary being a stammer the clung to me throughout my days, even until the year I entered university in 1984.

The common consensus among the speech therapists I saw over the years was that my speech impediment was related to anxiety, which had a lot to do with members of my family. My mother, without a shadow of a doubt, played a large role in manufacturing this condition, and later on the younger of my two sisters had an increasing influence on my speech impediment as well. It did, indubitably grow worse throughout all my schools years, (none of the speech therapists were able to contain or control my affliction).

I can confidently state that my stammer was the greatest defining element in my life; not because I perceived it as part and parcel of who I was, but rather I can declare that it became the instrument I would use, due to circumstance, fate, destiny, to examine people; how they interact with one another, affect the environment they're in, and conversely, how milieus affect people.

I couldn't possibly declare that this was a deliberate choice on my part, but over the course of time my speech impairment more and more served this role. I have not been inclined, as a result, to submit to peer-pressure at any point in my life; due to destiny, in a manner of speaking, I became instead an "outsider"; someone keenly interested in the lives of others; where, and with whom, they conduct their affairs; but not involved myself.

I developed a habit of creating various scenarios in my mind, a chain link of events that could possibly lead to a circumstance I observed. I would say I was striving to perceive things from a higher elevation, a tower of sorts, and from this fortress on high I imagined what lay beyond the horizon. My mind could take me anywhere; it danced with the wind, and told me of tales others would one day sing.

I developed a fondness for exploring nature, the fields, streams, brooks, and wooded areas, situated close to my home. I could say that even prior to my entering kindergarten I was consciously doing whatever I could to enhance my mind's capacity to appreciate the world that surrounded me.

Somehow, in some quadrant of my mind, I had the sense my life was meant for something special. I had no conception what that could be, but I was prepared to wait for the opportunity to discover what it was.

I recall sensing I was quite different from others, even while a young lad still playing with wooden blocks, Lego sets, and toy soldiers; not because I found it difficult to voice my thoughts and ideas due to having a stammer, but because I had the intuitive sense I was in possession of certain unique qualities I was unable to decipher or identify.

When I was at school, for the most part, I kept to myself; whether it was in the classroom, or the school-grounds outside. When I did join a game it might be, for example, "konkers", which involved attaching a nut to a string, then swinging it at the konker of your opponent; whomever cracks the opponent's konker first is named the victor, or "Rounders", for example, which some are more inclined to call cricket due to the bat used, (I think of it now as a form of baseball, and the only thing differentiating it from the North American form is the size, shape, and weight, of the object used to make contact with a small leather wrapped ball). I also enjoyed hop scotch, and being involved in a football match, (more commonly called soccer in America).

No matter the position I held on a team, or the type of game I played, I always tried to perform at the highest level I could. It didn't matter whether I scored, if I was noticed, or commended for my performance, and given a pat on the back; I simply loved the opportunity to try and do my best, taking myself to the limit, and then looking forward to taking the limit a bit further the next time.

I remember my days being carefree in Reading, and also the village we moved to slightly to the north when I was 6 years old, called Silverstone. I consider all my formative years to have transpired in Britain, prior to my entering my teens, when my family lived in Canada, and later Israel, then back to Canada once again.

I lived the life of a typical child while I was in England. I was allowed to stay outside for most of the day, but expected to be back for supper. I grew up fast, and I would say that by the time I was seven I'd learned all I required to take care of myself.

I can only recall a single occasion when I was growing up that my life was placed in any sort of jeopardy, and that happened on a stormy afternoon one summer's day when I was 5 years old. I was out in a field having fun with a neighbor about the same age as myself, and, unfortunately, it was that day I thoughtlessly decided to follow the lead of another, resulting in my slipping into a raging stream of water, and almost drowning; the series of events leading up to the incident are somewhat hazy to me now, which is quite possible due to the events happening in such quick succession, and also possibly due to my mind, for my own benefit, repressing memories.

What has remained with me, however, in regard to this incident was the concern expressed by so many in the neighborhood as to my wellbeing. Most believed I had experienced a very close brush with death. My companion was actually sucked beneath the surface of the water, and had to be rescued by firefighters. I escaped such a traumatic fate, all the while knowing full well it could have easily been me as well, and I just happened to be the luckier man on that particular day.

It was decided I didn't require being taken to a hospital, but I should be kept close watch on at home over the next couple of days to make sure there wasn't any residual shock, or trauma. Many of the neighbors rang our doorbell during that time enquiring about my condition.

I remember this all so well because it would apparently be the last occasion that I was able to note anybody having any degree of genuine concern as to my health, whereabouts, well-being, or even, as sad and pitiful as it may sound, whether I was dead or alive.

I would have to say my finest friend, and possibly the only genuine companion I had throughout my life · one involving, trust, loyalty, and sacrifice · was a dog named McDougal, whom I acquired as a pet while living in Israel.

I only had the opportunity to know him a couple of years, from 1978-80, because my family decided to abruptly leave this country; (I was given just two weeks notice). Due to not being able to bring McDougal back to Canada, I spent much of this time trying to find a suitable home for him.

Despite my best efforts, believing I had left him in good hands, I discovered just two weeks after my arrival in Canada that he was abandoned on the grounds of a kibbutz. I was never able to garner any additional information about what happened to him.

Strangely enough, I suffered the same fate as my beloved dog four years later. I had seemingly left no impression on those I had encountered throughout my life, despite the fact I used to brag about my ability to memorize a symphony after a single hearing, and when I entered university I knew more than every one of my professors; I had also been creating works of art for the pleasure of others since my days as a young lad living in Silverstone; regardless, I left this world in 1984 as if I had never set foot on the surface of this planet.

When I re-joined the company of Man some 23 years later, I discovered I would greet much the same treatment as I did before, although for different reasons, and though I believed it inconceivable, a more extreme version than I encountered before.

The behavioral pattern I incorporated into my life due to this ordeal was to focus on the good in any situation, and instill within myself the qualities of others I admired, while disregarding traits I consider less appealing. I have done this with members of my family, characters I read in books, parts played by actors in movies, and also my favorite musicians; those ingredients that make up the other person become my own.

Some might say that what I've described is a most peculiar series of events, but since I began working on the four volumes that comprise the book, "Love Is the Nature of Existence", nothing could possibly make greater sense to me.

The Holy Spirit, I have discovered, is what differentiated me from the people that surround me. Every moment I know that I am possessed with the greatest Love imaginable. My hope, wish, and prayer, is that many others, in the near future, by reading my books, will be fortunate enough to experience the same as myself;

God Be Willing!!

My audience will note within my writings numerous references to eastern mystics, Paramahansa Yogananda especially, and that I appear to have a fascination with the progressive rock group called "Yes"; the lead singer, Jon Anderson, in particular, who has also had a successful solo career, and at times has collaborated with a man from Greece specializing in electronic synthesizer music by the name of, Vangelis.

These people entering my life just prior to my going to live in Israel, while I was in Liverpool preparing for my Bar Mitzvah, which took place in a beautiful synagogue on Princess Road.

A relative I knew well told me he thought I'd enjoy the music of a group he thought was terrific called "Yes", and informed me they'd just released a new album, and persuaded me to go to a record store with him to check out the cover. When I saw the cover for the album "Going for the One" displayed in the store window I thought it was simply brilliant, and I decided, then and there, I would have to get to know the group better.

It was only close to three years later, when my family and I returned to Canada from Israel that I finally managed to get around to listening to one of their albums; this was solely due to a lack of funds.

I never had much cash on hand while in Israel. There was only one occasion when I happened to have the opportunity to buy some "personal" items, and this was due to working several weeks in a warehouse packing oranges into crates; despite putting in ten hour days, 6 days a week, I only managed to only earn enough money to buy a cheap chemistry set, a leather soccer ball, and a single music tape by the rock group "Queen".

I picked up the album "Close to the Edge" at a local library and within no time at all my mind was drifting into the cosmic realms hidden within the mysterious, enigmatic, lyrics written by Jon Anderson.

I must admit at the time I was like so many others, and found much of his writings indecipherable - "total mass retain"? It was simply due to finding the man so captivating, so intriguing, that I decided I would have to find the portal that would lead to the door that if opened would disclose the secrets I believed he held about life, the universe, the heavens, spiritual beings, and countless other esoteric, "occultist", matters.

I remember continually being made fun of by my friends at the time, the ones I'd play road hockey and football with after school, because I started to dress like him, and grew my hair past my shoulders, much as Jon Anderson appears on the inside sleeve of his first solo album, "Olias of Sunhillow", (this was a behavioral habit that began early in my life; learning about, then becoming, in a sense, the people I looked up to, admired, and wanted to be like; I became a consummate "method actor").

I eventually found the portal I was searching for a couple of years later when I bought the double album, "Tales from Topographic Oceans", originally released in 1973, and read on the inside sleeve a comment made by Jon Anderson about a footnote on page 83 of Paramahansa Yoganada's, "Autobiography of a Yogi"; even since I have been fascinated with mystics, yogis, Self-realization, and the search to find the secrets hidden within the mysterious, ethereal, realms of the unknown.

Silver in a Stone
Silver in the Sky

he day the Stagecoach thundered into Town, local folk couldn't help but stand and stare. It seemed as though a circus had arrived, containing maybe an old grizzly bear.

Hooves tread into the snow,
while the driver smiled, and tipped his fur
*   cap.*
Why was it here?
No one was really sure;
but peculiar noises and sounds were carried
*   in the air,*
in the wind that continued to blow.

Before the Town had been sleepy and
*   sedate.*
The Vicar hadn't yet risen to grasp his
*   bottle of wine.*
The Church bells were still quiet.
It was Sunday, and all was quite fine.

Newspapers were piled in a shop on a
*   corner;*

The Trinity Manifesto; Vol. I

waiting for the Town's people to saunter
    in.
It was still the weekend
so it took a while after sunrise for the day
    to begin.

The Pub, not far from the Tobacconists,
was hollow, and dark.
Hours before a crowd had cheered inside.
The dust and saw still lay on the floor,
along with the remnants
of what had taken place the night before.

In the cellar were canisters of beer,
beside bottles of whisky and gin;
to those who cared to tread through the
    owner's door,
this was a place where life never became a
    bore.

Lights were turned on within every home,
as the coach, and galloping horses, paraded
    by each one.
People wondered;
where on earth all this could have possibly
    come from?

A century before the sight of such would
    have been far from rare,
but, in this day and age,
few had the time, patience, or penny,
to acquire such a means of travel!

They'd been taught this was right by Mr.
    White.

The Trinity Manifesto; Vol. I

He was the Headmaster of a local School;
who barked commands with a hand held
    gavel.
A few would call Larry on their phone.
He'd come with his yellow taxi from
    Towchester.
His service was displayed on a large blue
    poster.

One would think
horses should be in fields,
stagecoaches in museums, or an old film,
a man wearing coat-tails and a fur hat,
belongs in a Dickens novel,
in a city, where a home might be described
    as a decrepit hovel.

What a sight to behold,
was this spectacle that hadn't grown old!

The past had come to greet the present.
How this could possibly be, is far beyond
    me;
but as I watch the stars twinkle in the
    sky,
the moon whispers as the clouds pass by,
it would seem that nothing more pleasant
    could
fill a magical night dream.

Did it actually occur,
or did gusts of wind uncover a hidden
    terrain?
To speculate more
one might cautiously refrain;

The Trinity Manifesto; Vol. I

but why lessen the wonder in a bowl
that seeps sand into the one below,
when living life to the fullest
should always be our eventual goal!!

Wind Carries the Petals of a Rose

 fter her swollen knuckled
hands had swept over a
pair of candles several
times,
she'd lift them to her face
to shield her closed eyes.

In a voice that
    was neither muffled, nor distinct,
    she'd say our Lord is blessed,
    as well as our world which is His
        Kingdom.

Heaven and earth
can be joined by a word we call love.
That being so,
    our quest should be to achieve an ultimate
        freedom.

The Trinity Manifesto; Vol. I

Many believe, and have earnestly
    experienced this to be true,
I, for one,
can honestly say I truly loved my dear
    grandmother.
Her passing often leaves me feeling
    despondent, and quite blue.

She was the only grandparent my fortune
    allowed me to know,
thus, she meant more to me
than the grandest present wrapped in the
    most exquisite bow.

I've asked myself;
did she keep her eyes shut so as to not see
    the light that flickered before her?
Or was she expressing how open she was
    to receiving the eternal flame within
    her?

If the two can be considered the same,
the heaven and the earth are governed by a
    sole Monarch,
in whom our trust should never wane.

The story above could be perceived as a
    lesson.
We have things we can learn from every
    person, situation, place;
even the sight of a single flower hiding in
    the shadows of a country garden.
All can be seen as a beautiful
act of glorious grace.

The Trinity Manifesto; Vol. I

Keats, the beloved poet,
whose imagination spanned across moors,
    streams, fields, and hills,
but mostly resided in a small room many
    generations ago,
once noted that;
"Truth is beauty.
Beauty is truth.
That is all we know.
That is all we need to know."
If we treasure such wisdom,
our world would never cease to glow.

Our struggles may appear to overwhelm.
Tomorrow may contain sorrow also pain,
but there is always hope when we believe
    we can be happy again.

Despair can dampen our spirit,
but as long as a flame exists that emits
    light,
our lives can expose something enormously
    bright.

My grandmother taught me all these
    things;
not by the words she said,
but by using her life as a means to be an
    example.
Since I've found my life to be far from a
    gamble.
Her gestures, wet kisses, laughing smile,
    and sweet hello,
were all the nourishment I needed,
along with her succulent homemade dishes
    that I couldn't wait to sample.

The Trinity Manifesto; Vol. I

Liverpool was once a harbor, then a port;
later it was bombed by a dark enemy that
*   left piles of*
brick, mortar, and rubble.
In bomb shelters people would cower as
*   they sat in a huddle.*

The sirens still ring in the ears of her
*   citizens to this day.*
History displays lessons we are not
*   supposed to forget.*
Future generations should listen to those
*   who have endured these things,*
to better understand what it is they are
*   seeing.*

Till this day many mix laughter and pain,
*   sweetness and sorrow,*
to form a humor few could possibly find
*   hollow.*
All entwine together to form a place that
*   is marvelously unique.*
Continually streams of people flood this
*   patch of ground,*
striving to reach answers to questions
*   they've desperately chased like a*
*   hound.*

My grandmother's house is contained in a
*   borough named Great Crosby,*
which is situated close to the shores of the
*   River Mercy,*
near a stretch of water large enough to be
*   called a Sea.*

The Trinity Manifesto; Vol. I

Within, between, betwixt, this cross
    section,
was the place my father grew up in,
and I also had the chance to share in the
    wisdom he'd been given.

Rose's home was a studio, in which I
    studied life,
and all it so generously has to offer.
I slept in her bed, played on her lawn,
shared time with relatives and friends,
none of which she found to be in the
    slightest a bother.
Here I learned to accept me,
and all I might possibly one day have a
    chance to be.
Spread over many rooms were relics that
    served as
symbols of times that had already passed.
They remain in my mind,
because I viewed them as monuments that
    were made to last.

My grandmother developed traits, and
    carried them all so well.
They were displayed in the manner she'd
    walk;
steady, sure, determined, strong;
things we must be sure we require if we
    wish to live long.

A face may act as a reminder that a smile
    may not be on display,
but within lies a heart
that is filled with the substance that can
    make us gay.

The Trinity Manifesto; Vol. I

I encounter so many sights, and sounds,
that remind me of my grandmother every
    day.

She departed from this earth many years
    ago, but, if you listen carefully,
you'll hear the sound of her presence still
    present within my soul,
and all that constitutes my essential being.
Look carefully, and you'll notice,
it is her essence you are actually seeing.

My laughter, smile, cheer, thoughtful
    glance, and casual greeting,
would not be as they exist today,
if it were not for my grandmother and I
    meeting.

I have now become aware that an
    assembly may occur in a Hall,
where there might be an occasion for
    people to have a Ball.
No matter the position in which a person
    may stand,
little, of any of this, can I find bland.

There isn't much I take seriously, due to
    the strength in my heart,
which leads to my regarding life as
    somewhat a lark.

People may come and go, hustle and bustle
    to and fro,
whistling a tune as they mow.
My grandmother kept herself amused by
    this show,

created by the specimen we call man,
while adhering to what the Bible says
    about eating a chunk of ham;
I must say, though, on her buttered toast
    she'd put a great deal of jam.

Her identity was sustained by her
    character that was determined to
    persevere,
and has since enhanced my ability to keep
    myself fully in gear.

Life, after all, is incredibly precious, and
    time, really, is all we've got,
therefore, is it really wise to place a value
    on objects such as
tables, chairs, clocks, or even an ocean
    sandbar?
I learned all these lessons well with the
    help of a person
I referred to as my Grandma.

Inspirational Birth Right

tar light, star bright;
why am I here, staring at
the moon?
Waiting to see if an
answer will come soon?

Through the leaves,
branches, the globe shines,
reflecting the light driven from the Sun.
Beauty surrounds, filling the air with
waves of golden heavenly fun;
yet, not far in the distance are those ruled
by the barrel of a gun.

I hear creatures, scurrying, between,
around, and over,
the refuge left on the forest floor.
In homes families stare at screens revealing
scenes full of hideous, despicable, gore.
Within their sight, given eyes open wide
enough,
is an entrance signified by a door.

Knock and a bird will sing.
Turn the knob, and an eagle will spread a
wing.
Push, till a gap is created, and your call
will be answered.
"What is it you need, tell me, and I will
gladly to you bring."

The Trinity Manifesto; Vol. I

*Seek first His righteousness, then all else
will be provided.
Words of wisdom, constructive criticism,
are required to be guided.
Flattery, conceit, contempt, bewilderment,
secure us to the earth.
Drifting till we descend,
eventually leading us to a pit of quick
sand.
There we fall,
to be submerged in our own despicable,
disgraceful, acts:
no one will be present to offer a helping
hand.
All was, is, will be,
due to the actions, deeds, words, thoughts,
perpetrated by you.*

*Hades or heaven,
is a choice we make for ourselves.
We can live in riches, with bitches, ghouls,
fairies, demons, or elves;
our sluggishness initiated by inertia brings
transformations to a halt;
instead awaken to the resounding echo
calling from
a ceremonial, memorial, bell.*

*The greatest treasures are
buried in the Truth that lies within you;
or the gifts, spirit, essence, soul, can
explode,
like merchandise left on a shelf displayed
to sell.*

The Trinity Manifesto; Vol. I

Good, bad, positive, negative, mighty,
    lowly, dull or sensitive;
a single correct path is all one requires to
    be of benefit.

Spiraling downward, continually
    ascending.
The deeper you go, the greater the darkness
    you see;
perpetually distancing yourself from the
    Truth.
A light can grow so bright, it can literally
    blind;
maybe then, inside is revealed the brilliance
    of the mighty Lord.
The people you meet,
the disfigurements you endure,
can be easily overcome by the salvation
    open to you,
which you can choose to greet.

Seek, and you will find.
The greatest are always of the utmost
    kind.
You may not recognize the Truth,
and instead interpret signs of hate,
but, eventually, when the time is right,
probably when you are alone,
and enjoying the sight of the distant,
    glowing, moon,
you'll realize the sights seen before were
    manufactured
by things within yourself that did reside.

The meeting of minds is equal, fair.
Sending, receiving, retrieving, feeling;

The Trinity Manifesto; Vol. I

growth can happen in spirit,
or dive resulting in an enormous upheaval.
Either way, it is necessary to avoid Evil.
Truth will explode in innumerable
   directions,
reaching our previous deluded, illusionist,
   reflections.

What is left is a space where nothing
   untoward can roam;
then upon an early morning horizon an
   orange will creep upward;
turning gold, yellow, then finally white;
leaving eventually nothing than can stop
   its rays.
No matter the distance, altitude, latitude;
land, stream, river, or sea;
each offers a place where you can
   tranquilly sit, and simply be.

Album Cover "Olias of Sunhillow"

The Trinity Manifesto; Vol. I

(Excerpt)

In the summer of 77, I travelled from Liverpool, where I had my Bar Mitzvah, to live in Israel.

My family and I arrived at Ben Gurion Airport, just outside of Tel Aviv, late one evening, and by the time we managed to leave the terminal, it was just past 2 in the morning.

Security was very tight in those days, as it is now, as a matter of fact, so every inch of our luggage was inspected before we could leave. One thing I remember, that struck me as being quite out of the ordinary, was what happened after I made a comment, (and this was after our papers, and bags, had been given clearance), about machine guns; what surprised me was my father's reaction; "Keep your voice down! Watch what you say!"

Frankly, I didn't notice anybody particularly alarmed, or concerned, about my, "off the cuff", comment. What had developed in my mind, however, was a suspicion that something wasn't quite right. I couldn't place my finger on it, but my eye, figuratively speaking, was latching onto something imperceptible that had a "dark" presence; another way of describing my circumstance was that I had a sense of foreboding; something ominous was in the air, lurking, and watching. I kept my mouth shut until we all stood on the sidewalk immediately outside the main terminal.

The air was warm, and the sight of palm trees all around was a pleasure to behold. The night, I thought, was surprisingly quiet, especially considering the fact I was standing in the midst of an international airport; then, all of a sudden, I realized the country I was in was a small fraction of the size of England, and would hardly register at all on the landscape of Canada, (the world's second largest country, then, and now). The change I found comforting; somewhat like finding yourself in a cozy chair that fits every curve of your body perfectly.

A large Mercedes taxi, containing several rows of seats, drew up in front of where we'd collected, and the driver asked us where we'd like to go?

"Ezorim", my father answered. This was news to me; I was under the impression we were moving to a town called, Netanyah.

I knew very little about Israel before our arrival. I was shown a picture of a street in Tel-Aviv, lined with palm trees on both sides; which quite impressed me; and that was about it The extent of my knowledge of the Hebrew language was, maybe, not even being conservative, a vocabulary consisting of no more than a dozen words.

I knew how to read Hebrew, but only with vowels, which was due a lack of familiarity with the meaning of words. I'd acquired whatever proficiency I'd obtained in the language by being a student for a couple of years at a Hebrew Associated School in Toronto prior to immigrating to Israel.

It was never explained to me how this interest in Judaism, Israel, and Hebrew, suddenly arose; I simply did what I was told to do. I am proud to say that although I garnered very high grades at the Hebrew School I attended, I have little comprehension of how I achieved this feat, due to making a habit of insulting my teachers, (I even referred to one as a "jackass" on several occasions). It didn't bother me in the slightest that I could be dismissed from class for such forms of conduct, (some might deem the expression, "stunts", to be more appropriate). In fact my absentee record for the second year at this school was 173 days.

I must admit that I did have the impression it was rather strange, to put it lightly, that neither of my parents construed such impertinence as a reason to impose discipline. In order to somewhat lessen the degree to which this reaction alarmed me, I managed, to a certain degree, to convince myself that as long as I passed my courses, (I, actually got Alephs and Bets, or As and Bs, in practically all my subjects), they believed I was doing all that was required.

I would say the primary reason I didn't bother to attend so many classes, was because I had no idea why I was there in the first place. I had never liked the idea of anybody telling me how things are, and what they mean; I would rather enjoy the opportunity of discovering them for myself. In fact, this is what I have always believed being a student is all about. What is the point of someone telling me, 2 plus 2 = 4? I need to figure out for myself that 4 is the sum of two 2s.

I found it quite ridiculous, actually, that I was expected to simply accept another person's interpretation of passages in The Bible, without being given the opportunity to question why the person perceives verses a certain way, or even how their perception of anything developed!

Our luggage was put into the trunk of a taxi; then we all found a seat, leaving still a few seats empty, due to the size of the vehicle.

The driver exited the parking lot, and before I was even aware it happening, we were headed north on what Israel would have considered at the time, one of its' major highways.

What struck my mind as being peculiar was the condition of this throughway for cars, (in contrast to what I'd become accustomed to seeing in England, no matter the region); there was a strip of gravel each side instead of a paved curb, and the paint used to separate lanes, and indicate its border each side; which was often hard to see due to the extent the colour had faded.

What stuck in my mind, however, was the, at times, complete absence of trees and green grass for vast stretches of time, or so it seemed to me; only sand was visible, or a collected body of it, commonly called a "dune".

I don't remember any one of us talking much during this trip. I imagined the others in the car, except for the driver, were witnessing, and thinking, much the same as myself.

The only other thing that seemed a tad peculiar to me was the absence of houses. Most, it seemed, lived in apartments, contained in towers that were either square, or slightly more rectangular, in shape, and very few were above a dozen stories tall.

At times the Mediterranean Sea could be seen lingering in the distance, not very far away. The water appeared flat; silently waiting, I thought, for a time to churn, clap, and splash, once again.

I must admit that what I found most odd was my own reaction to being in this foreign landscape I was entirely unfamiliar with. It was only due to having the opportunity to study a map while I was in Canada, that I knew Netanyah, (my father had explained to the driver that Ezorim was a suburb of this town, slightly to the south), was mid-way between Tel-Aviv and Haifa, two of Israel's three largest cities: I use the word large, while also recognizing this is a relative term, and London, England, would have easily swallowed all three of Israel's big metropolitan areas if they were collected and formed a single urban area.

I couldn't be absolutely certain, but, I believe, that in order to arrive at our destination, we spent less than a single hour in the taxi; which served as a reminder once again that Israel was a tiny strip of land in comparison to the two other countries in which I had resided till that time.

When we turned left off the highway, onto a much narrower road, and into the town of Ezorim, I can't say that I was in any way impressed with what I saw. Unlike the apartment blocks I'd seen on the outskirts of Tel-Aviv, the ones here appeared to be dirty; practically all the buildings I'd seen, thus far, had been covered with a pale colour, usually either white, beige, or some sort of cream-(ish) hue; a type of yellow. Buildings consisting of bricks, which is typically the case in England, was, as far as I could determine, a most unusual, if not rare, phenomenon.

Every single building I could see now was evidently in need of a good wash. I couldn't imagine at that time how such a level of filth could accumulate. I was pretty sure, despite Israel being in a tropical region, that it must, from time to time, experience a rain shower.

Litter was shattered in practically every direction I looked; garbage dumpsters were overflowing with trash; the most nauseating, and quite disturbing, sight was the appearance of dead animals sprawled across roads. I'd counted three prior to our arriving at the metal gates that served as the entrance to, what would apparently be, our new home; a segregated compound relegated for new immigrants, otherwise called in Hebrew an "Ulpan".

The decaying carcasses strewn across roads, covered with insects, with flies visibly hovering above, were those of dogs. It was impossible for me to fathom how something so disturbing, and utterly disgusting, could come about; despite the nauseating effect these unsavoury sights had upon my stomach, the people that lived in the apartments here, and hung their laundry to dry on lines that spread across balconies, were content with what they had, and had decided to live with such squalor, filth, and stench. I was, indeed, beginning to feel like a stranger in a strange land!!

When we all got out of the taxi, I can honestly say that I was appalled by the STINK that flooded my nostrils, and, quite literally, made my head spin. For the first time in my life I had the opportunity to recognize what death smelled like. The body of what appeared to be a German Sheppard was spread across the center of the road less than fifty yards from where we were standing; the guts were exposed, and tiny crawling creatures had collected to feast on the entrails.

I could only imagine, at first, that it lost its life due to a collision with a vehicle; but due to the condition of the surroundings in general, I wasn't comfortable concluding this had been the case. I considered there to be a genuine possibility members within the population of Ezorim were inclined to kill such beings that were once animated with life.

I made this judgement on the basis of the amount of trash that had visibly collected, and for some reason, evidently, had not been disposed of, and because the compound, that I was now discovering would be my next place of residence, was bordered on every side with a thick, iron, fence, held up with heavy, dark, metal poles, that were at least a dozen feet tall, and spaced approximately twenty feet apart. Who was being protected from what, and why? I asked myself.

My father pressed a button attached to the front gate that would alert somebody inside the compound as to our presence, (this is what the sign posted in both English and Hebrew above the buzzer indicated).

In silence, we waited for about five minutes, until an elderly man emerged from the doorway of a building maybe thirty yards within the compound; all the while, I continued to take in the state of squalor everywhere. I was beginning to grasp why all the foul smells were so awfully pungent. I was in the tropics now; any refuge left out in the open, would putrefy quickly due to the level of heat. The sound of flies buzzing around the dead dog not far away, was a reminder of this fact.

If hell had found a place on Earth, I was pretty sure it would look, smell, and sound, like the town of Ezorim.

"Shalom", the elderly security officer said once he reached the gate; then spoke a number of other words I had no idea the meaning of.

My father gave a response in Hebrew; the officer then looked at his clipboard, and appeared to scan a list.

A minute passed before the officer spoke to my father again; I couldn't understand a word at this point because my comprehension of Hebrew was so poor.

My father abruptly turned in the direction of my mother, and said; "This is unbelievable! He doesn't have our names down on the list. I've never come across such incompetence in my life."

The security officer spoke again, but in a much louder voice.

My father then said to my mother; "I can't believe this! He's saying that because he doesn't have our names on his list, we can't get in!"

"Say something! We can't just stand out here." My mother pleaded.

My father then spoke in Hebrew for a considerable length of time; until he appeared happy with the outcome, and the officer finally uttered a response.

My father turned to my mother, and said: "Good news! He'll find an apartment for tonight, and some mattresses to sleep on. Tomorrow we can go to head office, and an arrangement will be made to get a bungalow."

I was transfixed by this exchange of words; was all this possible, or even likely? My answer was to convince myself that the Staff inside the compound was as negligent as those living in the surrounding area that left their garbage to rot in the heat. The gate was finally opened, and we were allowed to enter.

At approximately four in the morning I found myself in an apartment on the second floor of a duplex, lying on a bare mattress in the same room as the four other members of my family.

I'd already concluded that things could only get better. What cheered me up quite a bit, though, was that the apartment we were in was clean, and from what I'd noticed so far, the Ulpan was not a place where litter would commonly be found on the ground. The lawns were neatly mowed, and the beds of flowers scattered about were beautifully maintained.

I also noticed, just as we were entering the compound, to the left, and next to the administration building, a parking lot filled with what I would describe as, luxury cars, (Audis, Peugeots, Saabs, and such like), along with, in stark contrast, a few cars that were not; most of which I would soon after discover were called, Escorts.

I had the impression, on the basis of what I saw, that the vast majority of the people here were quite rich, with only a few that were far less so, (my family would definitely fit into the latter category).

The following day my parents had an appointment in the Ulpan's administration building, and by early afternoon we were able to move our things into a two bedroom bungalow, quite close to the front entrance.

Until this could be co-ordinated, I took the opportunity to have a look around the Ulpan; believe it or not, I had no idea what an Ulpan was prior to arriving in this far off land.

Israel, to me, while in both Canada and Britain, was merely a photograph shown to me by my father of a four lane road, with two lanes separated from the other two by a strip of somewhat green grass; with palm trees planted an equal distance from each other within this strip.

The Ulpan had just one paved road, which was the major throughway, and was located close to the center of the grounds, bisecting the compound. Bungalows were located on either side of this road, and also a little further in the distance; two and three story apartment blocks, were located more on the outskirts of the Ulpan, closer to the fence that separated the new immigrants from the population of Ezorim.

I discovered a basketball court on the grounds, tennis courts, and a couple of soccer, (in England we call the sport, football), fields. The cafeteria where everybody collected for meals three times a day, with a snack between each, was located almost smack dab in the center of the compound.

I managed to have a word with a few people I came across as I was exploring the grounds, and was amazed by the variety of countries people had come from; France, Argentina, South Africa, the United States, and Britain, to name just a few. Without exception, they all spoke English well enough for me to say hello, introduce myself, and find out a little about them.

The bungalow that would serve as my home while we were on the Ulpan had two bedrooms, and a large, comparatively speaking, living room area, and a patio to one side. My sisters occupied one of the bedrooms, my parents the other; I had to content myself with a sofa to serve as my bed.

I discovered from others living on the Ulpan that, typically, people are allowed to stay six months, and during this time they are expected to; 1) learn Hebrew, either by attending the classes conducted on the Ulpan, or somewhere outside; 2) obtain jobs; 3) find suitable schools for their kids, and, of course; 4) find a place to live. While remaining on the Ulpan, the cost of housing, meals, and basic amenities, was covered by the government of Israel.

I must say, I thought this was a good plan; but I was still somewhat puzzled as to why I'd been brought to this country in the first place. My father had mentioned Zionism to me; but I had no knowledge at the time as to what this term meant; what he did say to me was that for Israel to continue to exist, more Jews needed to reside in the country; therefore, our presence alone was enough to make a difference, and our lives meaningful.

That all sounded wonderful to me; the only questions that remained in my mind were how, when, and why, did this "dream" arise? I was never provided an answer to such questions. Whatever information I'd been provided, which I've already noted, was deemed sufficient for my needs.

The first school I went to was called, "Shorashem", (in Hebrew, this word means "roots"). To this day I think of it as a zoo, filled with wild animals. Chaos was the order of everyday. Everybody seemed to go about saying, and doing, whatever they pleased, whenever they pleased.

Fights would break out in the stairwells, hallways, the playgrounds outside, even the classrooms of the school. The sight of a puddle of blood on the floor, or blood splattered across a wall, was not an uncommon sight. I was challenged to a fight on more than a few occasions while I attended this school, and, without exception, I found a way to avoid any form of physical altercation; typically, in a manner of speaking, I would talk my way out of it.

My days while attending this school consisted of bringing a book, written in English, to my classes, which I would quietly read while my classmates did whatever it is they did; acquiring a meaningful education wasn't something on the top, or even close to the top, of a list of things to do, as far as I was aware, for any of the students at Shorashem.

While I attended this school, I usually had two hours a day put aside to attend Hebrew classes; which turned out to be quite useless, because everybody was so much more advanced than myself; so I would simply sit, and appear to be listening, while comprehending practically nothing whatsoever.

I did, eventually, manage to become fluent in Hebrew, but not due to attending any classes, or participating in a program. I taught myself by creating a list of words every day that I would memorize the sound and meaning of. I also taught myself the tenses, past, present, and future, and the structure of sentences, (grammar). It took me about 6 months to become as proficient as, or so it seemed to me, any of the other students at Shorashem.

I can't declare that this was an extraordinary feat, because the language, in comparison to English anyway, is quite simple, and most people use a vocabulary of no more than around four thousand words on a daily basis.

I pretended that I hadn't learned the language so well, and so quickly, in order to continue reading my English books during class, and told others I managed to get the work done with the help of a tutor I saw twice a week.

I must say that during the time I lived in Israel, I was fortunate enough to become far better acquainted with the English language.

I repeatedly told both my parents about the persistent fighting I witnessed at the school, and the number of occasions others attempted to engage in a fight with me; but this appeared not to be sufficient cause to extract me from Shorashem, and find another school, or even take measures to make sure that while I was there I be safe.

All the while I endured this ordeal, the younger of my two sisters went to live at a school in the Negev, adjacent to a Kibbutz; her classes were conducted in English, and her fellow students were almost entirely from North America.

She shared a room with just one other person which, as far as I was concerned, was quite spacious. On the two occasions I travelled with my parents to this institution, located in the heart of the Negev, (the desert covering the southern portion of Israel), I can't say that I was able to witness, in regard to my sister, much reading or studying going on, but rather a preoccupation with her personal appearance; wanting to catch the eye of men while attending parties, dances, and other things of such nature.

The older of my two sisters, began studying at Tel-Aviv University, or so I was given the impression; which sounded a tad peculiar to me, because she was far from fluent in Hebrew, in fact, she knew less of the language than myself prior to arriving in Israel; therefore, how could she manage to pass courses? Her lectures were presented in Hebrew, and all her text books were written in Hebrew, as well.

It shouldn't have come as a surprise to me that 9 months after our arrival in Israel, she returned to Canada by herself. I was never given any prior warning that this would take place, and my father could only explain her behaviour, once she was already in Canada, and residing in the home of one of her friends, by mentioning that she had decided she'd prefer to be with her "friends".

My stay at the hell hole called "Shorashem" lasted a year: fortunately, during the summer break I attended classes at a school in Netanyah, in order to improve my Hebrew; and it was there that I heard about a school called "Ort". I decided, even prior to visiting the campus, (located on the outskirts of Netanyah in an industrial area), that it would, far more than "Shorashem", suit my needs, and more importantly, provide a safer place for me to attend classes, study, and be a participant in recreational activities.

It was only once I was formally a student at this school, that I became aware I was now a member of the finest High-school in all of Israel.

While I was making every effort to improve my education, and look after my safety, and well-being, my parents were looking into housing. On several occasions we travelled to view an apartment building under construction on the outskirts of Jerusalem.

I was informed by my parents they had obtained visual merchandizing jobs at a department store in the heart of what is called "New Jerusalem" prior to our coming to Israel, and this is why they thought it best we live in the city as well.

On each occasion we visited the building site, we were informed, according to my father, that the construction project would require two more weeks to be completed. While waiting to occupy the positions designated for themselves at the department store, they developed a window dressing business by doing the windows of stores in Netanyah, Tel-Aviv, and Haifa, among other places.

The story I was later told was that because the apartment in Jerusalem was taking too long to prepare, they lost their jobs at the department store, and consequently a three bedroom apartment was chosen in Kiryat Nordeau, (situated just south of Ezorim).

When we left the Ulpan after nine months, three months longer than was considered typical - waiting for the apartment in Jerusalem was used as the excuse for staying longer - the government provided all our basic furnishings; including dishes, pots, pans, cutlery, sheets, pillows, etc.; during the remainder of the time we stayed in Israel very little beyond what the government had provided was bought to decorate our home.

It was quite apparent to me at this point that something wasn't even close to being right. If my parents had acquired jobs at the department store prior to our arrival in Israel, this would represent a stable, secure, source of income; why wouldn't they just find an apartment other than the one under construction? There was hardly a shortage of available "living units" in and around Jerusalem at that time; and, of course; why, and how, would a department store hold jobs? If the positions were obtained while my parents were still in Canada, how did they manage to prove their suitability for such positions?

It became quite apparent to me that neither of my parents had jobs waiting for them in Israel, and I was the only one of their three kids making an effort to integrate, learn Hebrew, and create some sort of future for myself in this country.

I didn't know why I was brought here along with my family, but what I was sure of was that things weren't adding up, or making the slightest bit of sense, which, understandably, made me uneasy, and insecure about what the future held for me.

When we moved into the apartment in Kiryat Nordeau, I expressed my wish to have a dog as a pet. I assured my parents that I would take good care of it, and I would assume full responsibility for its health and well-being. I hadn't had a pet of my own before, and I simply stated that I really wanted a companion.

An ad was discovered, (or so I was told), it may have been posted on a local billboard, in a store, for example, or possibly a newspaper, I can't be sure, but the younger of my two sisters came up from her "school" in the Negev, and told me she knew about a litter of new born puppies, about two months old, in need of a home, and from a "friend", no less!

To be honest, I never ever bothered to question this story; which friend? Where? How? No name was mentioned. I would suspect, presently, that the only intention was to provide the impression that she, along with my parents, had a personal interest in making me happy.

On a dark summer night, similar to the one when we arrived at Ben Gurion Airport from England, the four of us, (the older of my two sisters had already left Israel to be with her "friends" in Canada), drove in my parents yellow Subaru station wagon, to a town just north of Tel-Aviv called Hertzelia.

I remember well the streets we drove through in this town before arriving at the house that held the litter of puppies in question. Unlike most urban areas in Israel, Hertzelia consisted almost entirely of houses. None could be - at least by the middle-class standards of Canada, and Britain, at that time - considered luxurious, but in Israel, when I was living there, merely having a house, of any sort, even a compact, one story, bungalow, meant you were considered among the privileged, and you probably had both a colour T.V., and a phone, in your house, as well – these were perceived as luxury items in Israel at that time.

It didn't take me long to decide which puppy I wanted; the one different from all the others. He had a light blond coat of fur, while the others had fur much darker.

He was placed in a cardboard box we'd prepared on the back seat of the Subaru station wagon, which had a thick towel inside to help make him feel safe and warm. As we made our way back to Kiryat Nordeau, the only thing that meant anything to me in the world was that I had a friend, a companion, someone I could take care of.

My father thought of the name "McDougal" for my companion. He told me he knew of a man many years ago who, for some undefinable reason, reminded him of my pet; a tiny dog, with big floppy ears, and had a shaggy coat of fur that grew so fast, it would sprout up and block his vision; so I had to trim it often, for him to see where he was going, and not trip on his own fur. The name given was really of no importance to me; what mattered was I had a dog I could call my own!

McDougal became my sole companion, whom I soon discovered would patiently wait for me until I arrived home from Ort. I took him for a walk every morning before I left for school, which was typically around 7:30 in the morning, and I would take him for a much longer walk around the streets of Kiryat Nordeau in the evening. Sometimes we would walk over the sandy dunes that separated the town I lived in from the Mediterranean Sea, until we reached the beach; there I'd take him off his leach so he could run freely, and dip into the water if he wanted.

As a family, my parents and I, (sometimes the younger of my sisters was included), travelled on the Sabbath – the work week was 6 days in Israel at that time, as it is today – to different parts of the country; the Galilee, parts of the West Bank, Haifa, Acre, Jaffa, to name just a few of the places we visited; without fail, McDougal would be included in these excursions, and appeared to enjoy the opportunity to explore as much as myself.

I never put aside much time to teach McDougal to heel, fetch, or sit on command, and McDougal showed little interest in learning such disciplines; regardless, I could pronounce him as the most obedient, devoted, pet, any person could possibly want, or expect.

Whenever I would go to a nearby store to do a bit of grocery shopping, I would attach McDougal's leach to a pole immediately outside. No matter how long I might be in the store, he would sit quietly, and patiently, for me to come out.

I remember one occasion, (fortunately, it only happened once), I walked out of a store, and completely forgot about McDougal. It was only several hours later, when I was seated at the dinner table, that someone became aware McDougal wasn't anywhere in sight; usually, he'd sit close to the table, waiting expectantly for someone to toss a scrape of food his way. Immediately, I left the apartment, and ran down the six flights of stairs to the ground floor, and sprinted across the street, only to find McDougal seated exactly where I'd left him, leach wrapped around a pole, silently waiting.

The stores had all closed by this time, (the Sabbath begins at sunset on Friday). When I began loosening his leach from the pole, his tail started flapping against the ground. Remarkably, he didn't appear to be in any distress, and was just happy I'd finally returned.

Since the time I had McDougal as a pet, I've learned that, typically, dogs like a bed of their own, or will tend to sleep at the end of their master's bed; McDougal appeared most comfortable when he was able to place his head beside mine on my pillow.

Anything I could do for my dog, (who had ears that reminded me of an elephant's), was a pleasure. My days were full of the gratification of knowing I could make living a better experience for another creature, and I was cognizant, as well, that whatever I was able to do was appreciated. McDougal was not a dog who was unafraid to express affection by washing your face with the lapping of his tongue, or jumping onto your lap wherever you might be, no matter the time of day.

I was surprised that despite his obvious dedication to me, that he refused to follow the simplest commands, such as fetching a stick, or staying at my side when I'd take him for walks; thus, one day, I thought I'd conduct an experiment I happened to invent off the top of my head. I can't say that it was related to finding out why he was determined to always do his own thing, but I wanted to find out, have some idea, just how intelligent he was.

What I did was toss a couple of small biscuits in a corner of the small balcony where we'd hang our laundry to dry, and then quickly find a place to hide. I did this seven times, only to discover McDougal remembered, in sequence, the places I'd hide, checking each one before looking for another place I might be.

I assumed he would track my scent, but for some reason he didn't want, (I believe), to do this; instead he chose the manner I have described to eliminate the possible places I might hiding. The apartment was small, so I don't see how he wasn't able to see me watching him as he was scurrying about from one place to another.

McDougal was indeed a mysterious animal in a great many ways, but there was one thing in particular I couldn't figure out while I had him as a pet, that does make sense to me now.

There was a buzzer in the lobby of our building people would ring, and an intercom in our apartment, so we had the option as to whom we wished to allow entrance in the apartment building. When I was inside the apartment, and the buzzer rang, McDougal, without fail, would run to the door, and start barking. If it was a member of my family, there was no barking, or commotion of any sort, when the buzzer rang.

A dog, as folklore tells us, and we sometime witness evidence of, is aware, can sense, (as do a lot of other animals), things people ordinarily cannot; an example of this phenomenon commonly seen in nature is animals seeming to have prior knowledge of an upcoming natural disaster, an earthquake, for example, and take appropriate measures to protect themselves.

This would appear to indicate, especially due to the regularity it occurs, that their "senses" are picking up "nuances" in the environment the normal human's six senses do not; I believe that is a fair, and logical, assumption.

McDougal was, and still remains, to a very large extent, a mystery to me. The one thing, I must say, I liked about him the most, was that I can't remember a single occasion when he came close to uttering a whimper of a hiss; how could he, when all he wanted to do was express his affection by covering your face with a wet, sloppy, kiss.

WOLF IN SHEEP'S CLOTHING

I see myself as a person at war, and the battle is against evil, and the weapon I am using to defeat my adversary is the pen. My aim is to dispense, as much as I possibly can, the truth in regard to the nature of my nemesis.

There is an expression which very much describes my present circumstance, and how I am able to do what I do; "Keep your friends close, and your enemies closer". I am quite literally in the trenches, on the battle field, surrounded by my enemy.

Lives are lost every day in the mine field deployed by those who are sick and depraved beyond belief; ask any of those who witness the same as I, and you will, practically without exception, not be told anything about what they have seen and heard, or a claim will be made that they have seen or heard nothing.

The logic behind this behavior, to make an analogy, is as follows; if I've been involved in the commission of a crime, and live off the proceeds of that crime, why would I say, or do, anything that would have a tendency to incriminate myself; for instance, mentioning any knowledge of a bank heist.

The various criminal acts detailed throughout my writings that take place in Canada, and are perpetrated by Canadians, are done in order to insure they may be able to acquire cash without having to do any actual work.

Canadians, generally speaking, are far too lazy to make the required effort to meaningfully educate themselves; as long as they are able to get whatever they want, whenever they please, then all is hunky dory, and it's yet another "good day".

Evil is narcissism; an obliviousness as to how your actions affect others, and the environment in general. I see it every day; for example, a person yapping on a cell phone in a ridiculously loud voice; something that would obviously be disruptive in a location designated for learning; but still such obnoxiousness transpires, without exception, every single solitary day on the university campus where I conduct my research and write.

It is plainly evident that the principle perpetrators of these acts are women; the sweet, lovely, specimens that smell so fine, look so enticing, and reportedly are made of sugar, and spice, and all things nice – a sheep in a wolf's clothing.

Within the animal kingdom, a common tactic used by a predator to capture and kill prey, is to approach with stealth until a distance is acquired that disables the prey's ability to flee; the distance will depend on such factors as the speed, agility, and stamina, of the predator, and the weapon(s) it has at its disposal; fangs, claws, for example, or both – picture a tiger lying in the bush, quietly waiting as a deer approaches a watering hole. The enemy and its weaponry are not detected by the unsuspecting deer.

The other animals that hope to share in the kill are hardly likely to intervene, or disrupt, the hunt while in progress; Canadians have been given a reputation of being complacent, and apathetic, for the same reason.

The economic-system labelled "globalization" has indemnified that "opposites" exist in the world. The "system" insures that over time this "opposition" will strengthen; extremes will become more apparent. A greater percentage of people will live in poverty, and a larger amount of wealth will become concentrated among a smaller number of people. Some will engage in grueling labor throughout the day in order to acquire the basic necessities of life, while a far smaller percentage will hardly expend any energy in order to acquire far beyond what is necessitated to survive.

I presently reside in Canada, and it's hard to note any genuine expenditure of energy to obtain a pay-cheque; irrespective, the purpose of the government, as far as the sleep walking population is concerned, is to make sure the economy grows, (the G.N.P. increases), and more jobs are created; "put people to work", should be the rally cry of the Canadian public; which is quite impossible, in the vast majority of cases, because one would have to develop the capacity to work, before any work could actually be done.

The shiftless, I-pod zombies, who inhabit this land, expect to get something while not providing anything even of remotely comparable in value in return; I like to call a spade a spade, therefore, I will declare that they are thieves.

This is has been openly declared by many members of the nation's three major political parties; at the same time, as remarkable, and unlikely, as a reasonable person would think, they like to pretend its hidden, and the problem will only be resolved once the culprits are tracked down, the extent of their crimes exposed, and they are held accountable for their transgressions to the fullest extent of the law.

There is now a lovely lady, a common person, who proudly declares she worked as a waitress, in a restaurant, (it's very important that this be made apparent, and that she isn't perceived as somebody who merely served coffee in a coffee shop), as a means to support herself while attending university, and therefore, someone, or so one is led to believe, in tune with the needs, wants, and desires, of the people, who has been designated as leader of one of the parties in the province I presently reside. She has made the claim that if she were given the privilege of becoming premier she would tackle the problem of $600 million that goes "missing" every year, (she's never claimed the full amount that goes unaccounted, only that this is the amount she is prepared to acknowledge).

She doesn't know where the money comes from, who might be responsible for "taking" it, or where it goes. She has, however, confessed that the matter is instigated by no one ever being held accountable for their actions, and because she is someone professing to have morals, she has promised that if she were elected premiere she would remedy the situation by appointing a minister; a "minister of accountability" – (Canada already has over three times as many ministers as England, yet has less than half her population).

This is all a load of poppycock nonsense; there's already a minister who would have all the information she's supposedly seeking; his/her title is the "minister of finance".

She tends to speak in a soft, melodious, voice, and wears such a warm expression on her face while saying such rubbish, hence, one might actually be tempted to allow oneself to be fooled into believing she actually gives the slightest damn about the crimes committed, and has any intention of doing something about them.

The truth is that her sole objective is to present a façade that hides the fact she's wearing a nylon stocking over her head, and this is done so that in case she's ever caught on camera while in the midst of perpetrating a criminal act, her identity won't be disclosed.

Canadians acquire the cash they so carelessly, and thoughtlessly, spend by stealth; take into consideration their weaknesses and strengths while conducting such affairs; they have far from a nimble mind, and have an overwhelming propensity to allow inertia to dictate their movements; in other words, unless someone has to do something, he/she won't do anything. The population, as a whole, therefore, preys on the weakest, and most vulnerable, and to insure the victim once captured is successfully slaughtered, the death will occur in an enclosed setting, and due to the illegality of the deed, as much as possible, there will be no record, or documentation, associated with the event.

"Love Is the Nature of Existence" describes the various tactics, methods, and devices, used to make sure such criminality proliferates. Due to the enormity of the present problem, and the extent to which it has spread, the deck of cards that constitutes the scaffolding that maintains the structure that is no more than a mirage to fool people into believing there is still a human civilization, must be swept the ground, and a new bedrock formulated to serve as the groundwork on which the creation of a culture is possible; which is indeed happening in our present day by such leaders as David Cameron and Barack Obama.

First and foremost what is essential is the enforcement of law and order; only then can people have the chance to live in peace, harmony, mutual respect and consideration; J. F. Kennedy once announced; "The very word 'secrecy' is repugnant in a free and open society".

I will next describe an incident which was caught on camera; consider the wider ramifications and implications of the act; I am speaking of an attempt to deprive a person of his life, which took place in a public place; first degree attempted murder.

An elderly man was pushed to the ground in one of the shelters in the city of Ottawa. I arrived at the scene approximately 5 minute after members of staff had presented themselves, and a call had been made for an ambulance to be dispatched at approximately the same time, or so I overheard one of the members of the staff claim.

It was evident that the man was having a full blown seizure; his skin was pale, and his breathing rapid. There are certain common sense things one should do if one witnesses such taking place, and there are numerous short, but informative, videos available on YouTube regarding the matter: in every way possible the two staff members, the paramedics, and the "police officer" on scene, did diametrically the opposite of what they were supposed to do.

He was not rolled on to his side; all those on the scene made no attempt to calm the man, to reassure him in any way; instead they made every effort to cause stress. He became visibly weaker, paler, and his breathing heavier, with every passing minute the death squad bombarded him with one redundant, superfluous, question after another.

Here are the minutes, and a camera recorded the whole incident; for approximately ten minutes he was badgered with questions from both members of shelter staff in regard to his present state of health, and medical history.

One might speculate that this was done in order to later relay the information to the paramedics; this, however, was not the case; as soon as the paramedics arrived all the same questions were repeated.

I was a few feet away from the scene, and requested approximately five minutes after the paramedics arrived, that his blood pressure be taken; in response I was asked, "Are you a doctor?"

I said, "Yes", meaning I have a doctorate; I was actually deeply troubled by what I was seeing, and believed I had a civic duty to do whatever I could to intervene in order to insure medical help was provided.

One of paramedics answered back; "Then you should have gotten here first". I then tried a bit of psychology, as a means to persuade them to do their duty, and said; "If you check his pressure you'll find its low", all the while quite certain it was dangerously high due to the unmistakable visible signs, (again refer to YouTube to watch short clips on the matters I'm detailing).

Over the following fifteen minutes the elderly gentleman, clearly in a state of distress, was pounded with questions; the copper, (official title, "police officer"), with relish joined in as soon as he arrived.

One should be very careful about brusquely grasping someone in the midst of a seizure; one of the paramedics decided to grab the back of his neck, and jerk it up, and only afterward bothered to ask whether he had hurt his neck recently; apparently, according to the elderly man, he had sprained his neck, and it was a bit swollen on one side; the exact place the paramedic was deliberately applying pressure to the further increase the man's level of stress.

It took approximately half an hour from the time the call was made for an ambulance till the man was taken out of the shelter on a stretcher; he was not lifted upon the stretcher, but grasped under an arm pit by one of the paramedics, and told to lift himself up.

Many of those who reside in shelters, due to "personal issues", are prone to seizures, and those whom one would expect are there to serve and help, do the exact opposite; the residents are malnourished, deliberated inflected with stress inducing situations, deprived of sleep, and proper rest; I have noted grapefruit being served on a regular basis in every one of the shelters; the staff at one of the shelters have thought it wise to reuse Styrofoam cups, and bowls; of course, making sure they've been cleaned in a dishwasher first – cleanliness is next to godliness, don't you know.

I briefly spoke to a "police officer" at the shelter where the elderly man was brutally attacked later on that evening, and asked this question; "How would you assault a man having a seizure?"

I deliberately made the question vague, so he'd ask for clarity; I next rephrased the question; "How would you assault a man having a seizure without touching him?" I could tell from the expression on the man's face he knew exactly what I was referring to. He replied by asking; "Are you saying the questions caused the seizure?"

I wasn't prepared to repeat the question, and get involved with his game. I responded by saying;

"By bombarding the man with a hoard of redundant, superfluous, questions?"

"Are you a doctor?"

"All I need is a little common sense to know it causes stress."

I'd hit the jackpot, and he knows precisely what I'm inferring; "Why was a police officer assaulting an elderly man?"

"I don't have to hear this", he said, before turning to his fellow officer, and asserting, "Let's get out of here", while literally pushing him through the doorway.

I followed the two outside, and requested that the officer present at the scene be charged, and informed him as well that a camera had captured the whole incident.

He told me he wouldn't do that. I then said; "Then you are complicit in the act." He replied, "That's right".

I pronounced him guilty due to his own confession. His last remark before hopping into his cruiser and speeding off, was; "You talk a load of nonsense"; such is the most common tactic used in Canada to hide their crimes; making sure witnesses are not heard, listened to, or taken seriously, because they have been deemed certifiable.

The truth is out there, it's obvious, and "Love Is the Nature of Existence" is intended to remove the twig that's clouding the vision of some, so that others can have the log removed that blocking them from perceiving even a smidgen of reality.

"Evil can only exist,
when good people do nothing to stop it."

There is a method one can use to measure the degree to which a civilization has developed a culture, and that is the extent to which the "advantaged" help the "disadvantaged", the able assist the disabled, the rich provide to the poor; which reminds me of a famous line spoken by John F. Kennedy during his inauguration speech; "Ask not what your country can do for you, ask what you can do for your country." The gesture made by one of his hands at the time indicates he meant this applies to everyone.

Canada is a country seeping with wealth; more money flows in than most apparently know what to do with; but still the population persistently feeds on its own citizens, behaving like a herd of savages waiting to devour the vulnerable, weak, and deprived.

Seniors across every quadrant of this country are particularly vulnerable to scavengers depriving them of their belongings. The government manufactures legislature to insure those who exploit, rob, maim, and wound, seniors, ultimately leading to their early grave, may have no fear of legal recrimination

The law of reciprocity is a foreign, strange, concept to practically all Canadians; even the ability to question how wealth arrives in this country is, for the most part, an irrelevant, inconsequential, detail in the minds of practically all. Once something lands in their hands, it is used solely for their benefit practically immediately; which is indicative of a mind operating in accordance with the "pleasure principle", and, therefore, lacking cultivation to such an extent only behaviour akin to that of a 5 year old is possible.

Within the wild kingdom predators commonly prey on those who are separate from the herd, possibly due to illness, a handicap, or perhaps circumstance. It is not uncommon, however, among the "higher primates" that females, the young, as well as those less agile, are protected by the strongest within a population. A human society that has developed a "culture" should display similar characteristics. Canada, on the contrary, consists of a population that rubs salt, figuratively speaking, into any exposed wound or handicap; this is particularly prevalent among the elderly.

Every one of Canada's provinces has its own health care system, and each is designed to make sure seniors cannot obtain the services, products, and medications required to sustain their health, this is particularly the case in regard to ailments commonly associated with aging. Canada does this in a manner that is exquisitely easy to identify; to provide an example, if a combination of three medications is required to treat an illness, at least one will **not** be covered under the provincial health care plan. This insures the senior is actually deprived of any affective treatment, while gouging his pockets at the same time. The ultimate goal is to hasten the death of the elderly, while as large a portion possible of their savings winds up the government's coffers.

The execution of such endeavours can only be labelled as diabolical, and reflects the general disposition of the public. The contribution seniors have made throughout their life to the economy, and the benefits they're entitled to as a result, mean nothing to those not facing the same circumstance. For the most part, as well, that which the elderly have managed to learn throughout their life is of trifling importance to younger generations, who, I'm sad to declare, view them primarily as money vaults they have access to as they please. It's not uncommon for men and women of university age, for example, even those with full time employment, to live in their parents' home for "convenience sake".

A common practice is that when tables turn, and either, or both, the parents require assistance from their offspring, the time is deemed appropriate by the young ones to find alternate living arrangements.

Such a mindset does much to explain why students of all ages debilitate themselves by not being able to consider the possibility another person's opinion may hold greater weight than their own. The common contention today is that there is no "hierarchy" in schools, which, as far as I'm concerned, drastically minimizes the possibility of any meaningful learning taking place.

When I look around the population of the university campus I frequent on practically a daily basis, I can't help but recognize how the level of maturity of the majority has been radically stunted; it is not an uncommon to witness their content, literally, to sit in their own filth; the mud from the shoes, and the remnants of the food they gobble like pigs and falls on their clothing, as well as the furnishing they recline on. The younger generation is also of the persuasive disposition to believe each is the most important person on the face of this earth, and no sacrifice is too great if it can add even a moment's pleasure to their life.

All the while the elderly in Canada are systematically cut down in their tracks, and the government permits this cruelty to exist on a scale that is difficult to conceptualize. There are, to illustrate my point, "homes" for seniors everywhere, and almost without exception, there are ongoing occurrences within each of residents being abused, robbed, and beaten, by those whose job it is to take care of them. The government elucidates that it is unable to effectively deal with the problem due to a lack of inspectors. Another way of viewing this brutality is that the government is aware of the travesty of justice, and has decided not to take the necessary measures to remedy it.

Love Is the Nature of Existence
VOLUME I

The Trinity Manifesto

Nigel Shindler

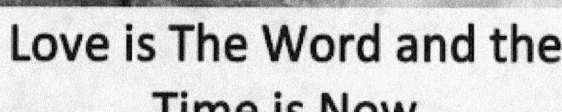

Love Is the Nature of Existence

VOLUME II

Love is The Word and the Time is Now

Nigel Shindler

*Love
Is the
Nature of Existence*

The Eternal Journey

The Trinity
Manifesto

LOVE PEACE
PRACTISE UNDERSTANDING

Nigel Shindler / Trinity Manifesto
Productions

Email; trinitymanifesto@gmail.com
Twitter; @NigelShindler
Google; NigelShindler

"Love Is the Nature of Existence"
is available on Amazon, and bookstores everywhere.

www.ingramcontent.com/pod-product-compliance
Lightning Source LLC
Chambersburg PA
CBHW060233290526
45789CB00001B/27